Mandalas to Crochet

Mandalas to Crochet

30 great patterns

Haafner Linssen

Search Press

A QUARTO BOOK

Published in 2016 by
Search Press Ltd
Wellwood
North Farm Road
Tunbridge Wells
Kent TN2 3DR

Reprinted 2016

ISBN: 978-1-78221-389-5

Conceived, designed and produced by
Quarto Publishing plc
The Old Brewery
6 Blundell Street
London N7 9BH

QUAR.CRMA

Senior Editor: Lily de Gatacre
Art Editor and Designer: Jackie Palmer
Pattern Checker: Therese Chynoweth
Photographers: Phil Wilkins (studio),
    Nicki Dowey (location), Simon Pask (model shots),
    Haafner Linssen (pp 8, 9, 18, 19)
Illustrator: Kuo Kang Chen
Proofreader: Julia Shone
Indexer: Helen Snaith
Art Director: Caroline Guest

Creative Director: Moira Clinch
Publisher: Paul Carslake

Colour separation in Singapore by Pica Digital Pte Limited
Printed in China by 1010 Printing Limited

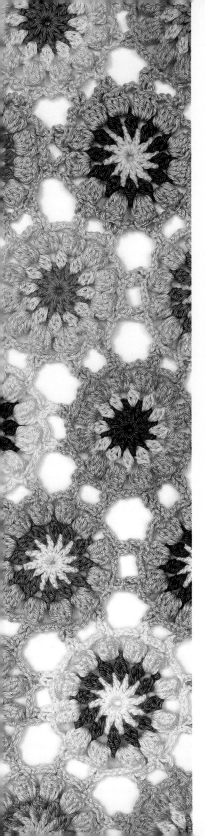

CONTENTS

ABOUT THIS BOOK

The heart of this book is the mandala patterns, but you'll also find so much more. The book is divided into three chapters, starting with essential information for before you start crocheting, then the mandala patterns and finally seven lovely projects to take your work to another level.

Before You Begin (pages 10–25)

As much as you might want to dive straight into the tempting mandala patterns, it's important to spend a little time in this section of the book, even if you are an experienced crocheter. In here, you'll find important information about the charts and patterns that you will encounter later in the book, as well as tips for how to make your mandalas perfect. A handy 'Crochet Refresher Course' is also included, which runs through how to perform the most essential crochet stitches and techniques.

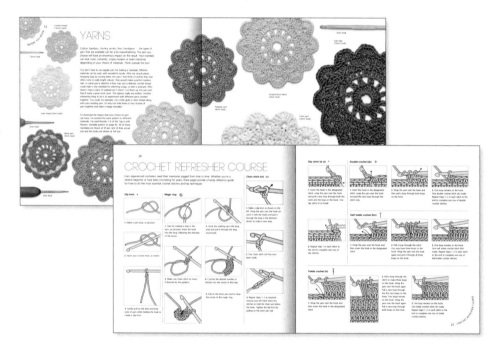

Mandala Selector (pages 26–35)

Don't know which mandala pattern to choose? Turn to this section and spend a little time looking at the stunning large-scale photographs of the mandalas side-by-side, and soon you'll find one leaping out at you. Be inspired and find the mandala that is right for you, or get ideas for shapes and colours that work really well together.

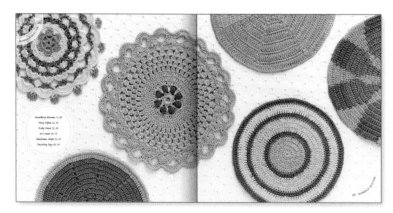

Mandala Patterns (pages 36–105)

The heart of this book is the 30 beautiful crochet mandala patterns, which are accompanied by large charts and beautifully photographed finished examples to help you along your way. The mandalas are divided into four groups to help you choose where to start: 'Basic', 'Classic', 'Flowers' and 'Something Special'. Turn to pages 102–105 to find some unique and beautiful borders that you can add to your mandalas.

Read this First! Turn to pages 16–17 to read some important information about different options for beginning your mandala, as well as how and where you start and end each round. The choices you make can have a big impact on the finished mandala, so take some time to consider all the options before you begin.

The hook size and approximate finished diameter are listed here. Mandalas made with a 3mm hook are made with DK yarn and those made with a 3.5mm hook are made with 4ply yarn

The group that the mandala belongs to is listed here

Anything important that you need to know before you begin can be found here

Beautiful photographs show you the finished mandala

Each chart has a segment shown in the colours of the finished example. Focusing on this section will stop you from feeling overwhelmed by the large number of repeats, and keep you on track

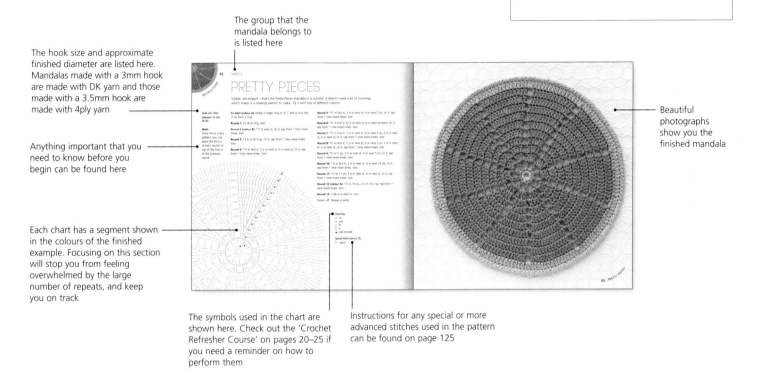

The symbols used in the chart are shown here. Check out the 'Crochet Refresher Course' on pages 20–25 if you need a reminder on how to perform them

Instructions for any special or more advanced stitches used in the pattern can be found on page 125

Here you'll find a thumbnail image of the mandala design that this project is based on

Projects (pages 106–123)

Mandalas are beautiful on their own but what else can you do with them? This section will provide you with the ideas, instructions, charts and construction diagrams that you need to turn your crochet mandalas into beautiful and unique home and fashion accessories.

Turn to pages 124–125 for a list of the symbols and abbreviations used in the book.

WELCOME TO MY WORLD

My name is Haafner and I'm a maker, designer, blogger and – of course – crocheter. I'm based in the Netherlands but I love to travel and can often be found exploring other countries.

I draw my inspiration from everywhere: flowers, nature, books, art, an unexpected street corner, vintage textiles, tiles, textures and colours! Anything can spark an idea for a new design. I hope something of my love for pretty and quirky things shines through in these mandalas.

For me it's encouraging that a craft like crochet connects people globally. We share patterns and inspiration, and often enjoy and like the same things. The appreciation for creating and the handmade crosses boundaries that otherwise often divide people. I'm very excited about the revival of and new esteem for the craft movement that is currently happening.

I studied art and literature, which strengthened my own appreciation of aesthetics. A couple of years ago I picked up a crochet hook and never put it down. It's such a versatile technique. With just a few simple stitches you can create something stunning. Crochet stitches can also be intricate and delicate. Crochet allows you to create amazing and tactile textures. Personally, I love to explore all kinds of stitches and techniques, so you'll find a variety of stitches in the patterns in this book.

My love for crochet is closely connected with my love for beautiful yarns. I'm sure many of you can identify with that!

It's a wonderful thought that you are holding my first crochet book in your hands. My goal was to make a book that is attractive for both the beginning and the experienced crocheter. I hope you'll enjoy making these patterns as much as I enjoyed designing them for you.

Happy crocheting!

PS If you are on social media, do connect with me and share your mandalas! Or visit me on my blog, byHaafner.

Haafner

Round and Round: A Short Introduction to Mandalas

'Mandala' is the Sanskrit word for circle. Nowadays, especially in arts and crafts, the term mandala is used as a generic term for any circle or round motif, often with a radial balance.

In Hinduism and Buddhism, mandalas have a ritual role, representing Buddha or even the universe. The different parts of such a mandala have a symbolic meaning. For instance, the outer circle often symbolises wisdom in Buddhism. Ritual mandalas can serve as an aid to meditation and, on some occasions, monks work on one mandala for weeks, only to destroy them ritually as a symbol of impermanence.

In recent times, mandalas have become increasingly popular around the world for secular purposes. They can serve as a creative outlet and for mere decoration. The process of crocheting a mandala is a relaxing, sometimes even meditative, activity.

Where it concerns contemporary crochet, the term mandala is widely used for circular motifs. Often there is not a sharp distinction between doilies and the more lacy mandalas.

9

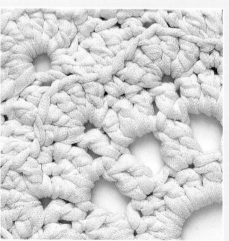

It's tempting to just grab your hook and go, but before you start your first mandala project, it's worth having a read through this section of the book. Here, you'll find information about what to expect from the patterns and charts in this book, advice on how to achieve the perfect mandala and a handy refresher course in case you need a quick reminder on some of the crochet basics.

BEFORE YOU BEGIN

Crochet thread
(1.6mm hook)

1.6mm hook

YARNS

Cotton, bamboo, chunky, acrylic, thin, handspun … the types of yarn that are available can be a bit overwhelming. The yarn you choose will have an enormous impact on the result. Your mandala can look rustic, romantic, crisply modern or even industrial, depending on your choice of materials. Think outside the box!

You don't have to use regular yarn for making a mandala. Different materials can be used, with wonderful results. Why not recycle plastic shopping bags by turning them into yarn? And think of clothes lines that often come in really bright colours: they would make a perfect outdoor mat. A coarse jute is ideal for a floor mat, but a delicate crochet thread could make a tiny mandala for adorning a bag, or even a postcard. Who doesn't have a stack of washed-out T-shirts? Cut them up into yarn and they'll make a great stool cover. The options really are endless. Another interesting thing to do is to experiment with different yarns worked together. You could, for example, run a little gold or silver thread along with your working yarn. Or why not hold three or four strands of yarn together and make a mega mandala?

To showcase the impact that your choice of yarn can have, I've worked the same pattern in different materials. I've used Rounds 1–6 of the 'Say it with Flowers' mandala pattern on page 82. All of these mandalas are shown at 50 per cent of their actual size and the hooks are shown at full size.

Linen thread (2mm hook)

2mm hook

Hemp yarn
(3mm hook)

3mm hook

Bamboo yarn
(4mm hook)

Linen/cotton blend
(4mm hook)

4mm
hook

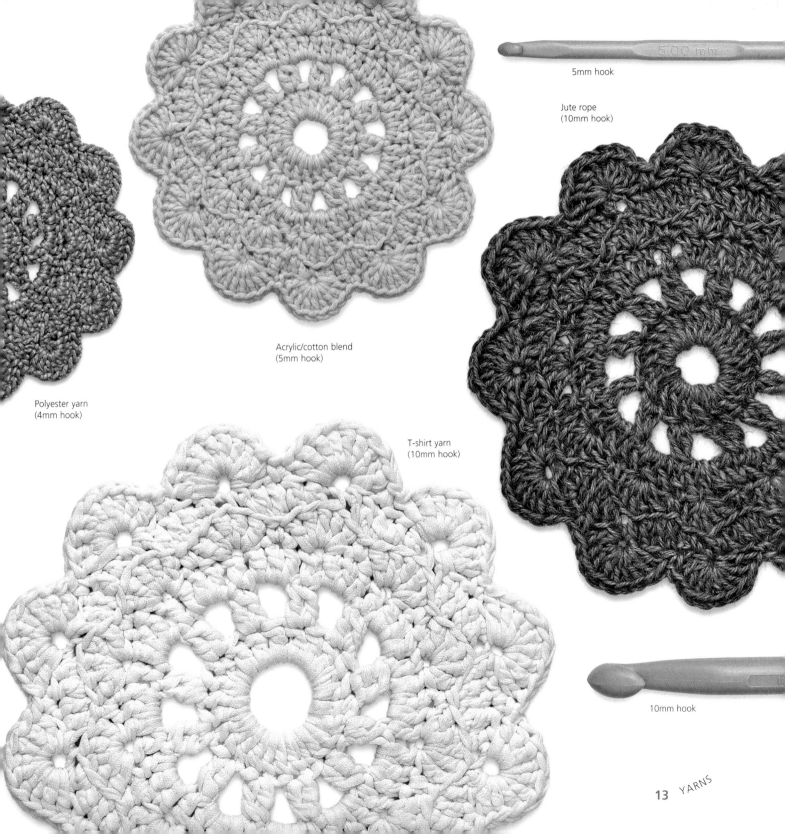

Polyester yarn
(4mm hook)

Acrylic/cotton blend
(5mm hook)

5mm hook

Jute rope
(10mm hook)

T-shirt yarn
(10mm hook)

10mm hook

COLOUR ME HAPPY

What a difference colour makes. Most of us have our personal likes (and dislikes!) for certain colours, and many of us find ourselves grabbing the same colours time and time again – even if we promised ourselves we'd try something different this time. Other crocheters don't have a strong colour preference or are still working out what their favourite colours and colour combinations are. Sometimes you'll like a colour just because of the memories it evokes and, of course, preferences can change over time: they'll change as you change, and they'll change with fashion.

Experiment with Colours

Mandalas are perfect for both discovering your personal palette and for exploring new ones because they are small projects in which you can use any and every colour you like. Here, we'll have a closer look at some different colour schemes, including monochrome, pastels, brights, muted and variegated. It's important to remember that sometimes a colour that you don't really like on its own might work perfectly combined with your favourite colours and help them to shine.

To showcase the impact of colours, I've worked the same pattern in different colour plans. I've used Rounds 1–6 of the 'Say it with Flowers' pattern on page 82. To be able to make an optimal colour comparison, I've used mercerised cotton for all these mandalas and a 3mm crochet hook.

Create a Colour Plan

Your colour choices are not just about which colours you choose. Note that I did not only use different colours for each of these mandalas, but I also used a different colour plan with regard to where I changed colours. Varying where you change colours will ensure that your work has a completely different look.

Compare, for instance, the pink, white and brown mandala (A) with the black and white mandala (B).

In A, Rounds 3 and 4 are the same colour, but 5 and 6 are worked in two different colours, giving Round 6 the effect of a picture frame: it 'closes' the mandala.

In B, Rounds 3 and 4 are worked in the same colour, and Rounds 5 and 6 are worked in the same colour. This way, Rounds 5 and 6 mirror Rounds 3 and 4. It almost seems that, instead of four curvy rounds, there a two big curvy rounds.

Mandala C (the bright pastels) uses a new colour every round, creating a completely different mandala. There is less coherence between the rounds than in other designs, but the effect is rather cheerful and has a retro appeal.

Look closely at all the mandalas on these pages and see how colours and the pattern of colour changes have a huge impact on the overall design.

A. Brown and pink hues form a scombination with a lovely, vintage vibe

B. Together, black and white make a bold and always classy impression

E. These blues will never give you the blues. Different hues of blue tend to combine perfectly with one another

F. These muted pastels give a very different effect from their bright counterparts (C), and add a certain elegance

C. Bright pastels give this mandala a cheerful, fifties appearance

D. An all-white piece is a guarantee for a stylish look – here, it's combined with just a touch of silver

G. Red and pink is an effervescent combination that gives an extra zing to your work

H. Variegated yarn demands your attention and gives energy in return. It is best combined with a monochrome yarn

READ THIS FIRST!

We have strived to make the written patterns and charts in this book as simple and clear as possible by omitting any confusing redundancies, and depicting charts in a way that doesn't make you lose count while crocheting. The information and tips here will help you to get a good understanding of the patterns you'll encounter in the rest of the book, and the choices you have about how you crochet your mandala. We recommend you read them before picking up your hook.

How to Start

In this book we always give you two options for starting your work. For each pattern, you can choose whether you'd like to start with a magic ring or with a ring of chains, secured with a slip stitch. There is no preferred method – try them both and pick the one that you like best. For each pattern, we indicate the number of chains needed for a ring.

Note that all of the charts in this book show a ring of chains, but you can simply substitute this with a magic ring if you like. The chart symbol for a magic ring is shown below for reference (but note that this symbol can vary).

Turn to page 20 for step-by-step instructions on how to work both of these starting methods.

 Ring of chains: Crochet the indicated number of chains and close them with a slip stitch to form a ring.

 Magic ring: Look out for the magic ring symbol in crochet charts that you find online and in other publications.

On the Go

Just as you have options for how to start your mandala, you also have options for how to start each new round. Our preferred method is to use what's called a standing stitch because it gives you a seamless start to the round. There is no crochet symbol or abbreviation for this and it's unlikely you'll see it specified in a pattern, but it's a great technique.

As there's no standard crochet symbol for a standing stitch, for clarity in the charts in this book we depict the start of rounds as shown on the example below.

You will often see the abbreviations st dc, st tr and st dtr used to denote standing stitches in crochet patterns. In this book we have not used these abbreviations as you might choose to use chain stitches instead of the standing stitch method to start your rounds.

It is entirely up to you whether you start with a standing stitch or you choose to start with a series of chain stitches: one chain for a double crochet, two for a treble crochet and three for a double treble crochet.

If you prefer to use chains at the beginning of a round, we strongly recommend making two chains in place of a treble crochet, instead of (the more common) three chains. Two chains will blend in nicely, whereas three chains will leave a visible join.

See page 23 for instructions on how to work standing stitches.

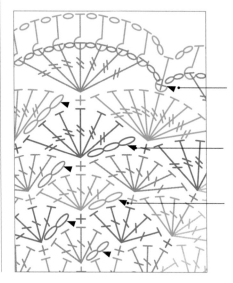

When the first stitch of a round is a double crochet, we show a regular double crochet stitch

When the first stitch of a round is a double treble crochet, we show 3 chain stitches

When the first stitch of a round is a treble crochet (or a special stitch that includes a tr, such as a popcorn), we show 2 chain stitches

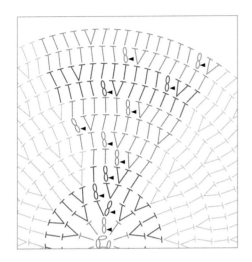

Where to Start a Round

So you've decided how you're going to start your new round, but where do you do it? In the charts in this book, we've almost always shown the first stitch of the round as not being worked directly on top of the first stitch of the previous round, but slightly staggered. If you prefer to start the round on top of the first stitch of the previous round, then you can certainly do that. See also 'Crochet a Perfect Mandala' on pages 18–19.

Notice how the arrows indicating the start of each round and the chain stitches (or standing stitches) that begin each round are staggered, and not stacked up on top of each other.

Joining a Round

You will often see the instruction 'join' at the end of a round. The most common way to join a round of crochet is with a slip stitch. However, the other option you have is to close the round using a needle. This is my preferred method as it gives an invisible join. Check out the instructions for the two methods on pages 24–25, give both a try and then use whichever method you prefer for joining your rounds. See also 'Crochet a Perfect Mandala' on pages 18–19.

Charts

You'll notice that the charts in this book are segmented, with just a section of the chart popping out in colour. Why have we done this? Well, because this way they are so easy to use.

When you're using a 'regular' crochet chart and working in rounds, it can be challenging to keep your place and get a sense of where the pattern repeats lie. The last thing you want to do is lose track of where you are in the pattern, especially with some of the larger mandala patterns. Also, big charts can look really daunting, and can make you think that a pattern is too complicated for you to tackle. Trust me: it's not! The segments break the pattern down into manageable chunks.

By following a segmented chart, you don't have to follow along the entire round, trying to keep track of your place. You can see where repeats start but still get a sense of how the repeating pattern fits into the full mandala.

Coloured segments show at least one pattern repeat of each round so that you only need to focus on a small area

The rest of the chart is shown in grey so you can still see how the mandala fits together

Early rounds with few repeats are shown entirely in colour

CROCHET A PERFECT MANDALA

It takes relatively little time to create a mandala. Therefore, it really pays to put attention into the little details. They will make the difference between an 'okay' piece and a small work of art. These tips and tricks will help you to make a perfectly round, perfectly polished mandala that you will be really proud of.

In the previous section, we ran through the different options you have for how you choose to crochet your mandala: how to start, where and how to begin new rounds and how to join a round. In all of these instances, the option you choose is entirely up to you and what you prefer and are most comfortable with. However, there are some options you can choose that will do more to ensure that your circular motif really is a circle. Consider trying out these options for your mandalas to get the perfect finish.

Below, the mandala on the right was created with 3 chain stitches to begin each round. Each round begins and increases in the same place and is joined with a slip stitch. The mandala on the left shows the result if you start each round in a new place, using standing stitches, and join each round with a needle. Note the difference.

Starting Seamlessly

Where and how you begin a new round is important. To create a perfect looking mandala, don't work the first stitch of a round on top of the first stitch of the previous round – work every first stitch somewhere else instead. This will ensure that the the joins are spread out and blend into the rest of the pattern – you won't have one particular area where all the joins line up and stand out. This is especially the case for solid circles, such as the 'Handsome Hoops' mandala on page 42. For lacy patterns, this is less important as the joins will be much less noticeable, for example with the 'Leaves and Lace' mandala on page 78. Starting each round at a new place also means that your mandala will stay round, rather then developing corners.

Similarly, using a standing stitch at the beginning of each round, rather than a series of chain stitches, will help you to achieve that truly seamless look.

Invisible Joins

In the previous section we discussed the different options you have for joining a round. It really is down to your personal preference and the slip stitch join is more common, but let's think about the impact your choice will have on your finished mandala. For some patterns the slip stitch join is absolutely fine. As with the position of your joins, this choice will have less impact on the more lacy patterns, such as the 'Lovely Lace', 'Oriental Lily' and 'Leaves and Lace' patterns (see pages 58, 76 and 78).

For other patterns, however – in general the more solid ones – a slip stitch will create a visible, less attractive join. For those patterns, it really will create a much prettier, more polished result if you use a needle to create a seamless join. See page 25 for instructions.

Bump created by using a sl st to join the round instead of joining with a needle

Gaps created by using ch 3 as a starting tr. Ch 2 would be better, and a st tr even better.

Visible line created by stacking increases

Corner created by stacking increases on top of one another

Increasing Rows

The basic principles of crocheting a circle mean that you have to increase every round with the same number of stitches. This way your circle should stay flat and look perfectly even. In general, a circle made up of double crochet stitches will begin with six stitches in Round 1 and then each subsequent round will increase by six stitches. So, 6, 12, 18, 24 and then up to 30 stitches in Round 5 and so on, with the increases spread out evenly around the mandala.

A circle made of treble crochet stitches will often begin with a Round 1 that consists of 12 stitches, which means that each following round will increase by 12 stitches. So, your first five rounds would be 12, 24, 36, 48 and then 60 stitches in total per round and so on, for as large as you want to make your mandala.

You can easily deviate from the standard number of stitches as long as you keep increases per round consistent. For instance, if your treble crochet circle starts with 16 stitches in Round 1, each following round will increase by 16 stitches: 16, 32, 48, 64 and 80 stitches in total per round and so on. Just make sure that the centre of your work is slightly bigger by making a wider magic ring or crocheting more chains.

Keep Your Circles Flat

Every crocheter has probably experienced it: your work unintentionally starts to ruffle (become too loose and ruffled at the edge) or to cup (form into a cup shape or lift up at the edges). Here are some tips to help you solve these problems.

If your work starts to ruffle, it means that the outside rounds are too loose, so try one of these options:

- Start your work by making a wider magic ring or by crocheting more chains in your beginning circle.

- Switch to a smaller crochet hook.

- Depending on the pattern, you can omit some stitches – chain stitches are often the best option.

- If the pattern calls for you to skip stitches, you can skip an extra stitch.

If your work starts to cup, it means that the outside rounds are too tight, so try one of these options:

- Start your work by making a smaller magic ring or crocheting fewer chains in your beginning circle.

- Switch to a bigger crochet hook.

- Smuggle in a few extra (preferably chain) stitches.

- If the pattern calls for you to skip stitches, you can skip fewer stitches.

Ruffling

Cupping

The Finishing Touch: Blocking

For most mandalas it is essential to block them after making, and there are many techniques you can use. Circles can be a bit tricky to block and, if it's not done right, your circle can end up having corners.

An effective and simple blocking method for mandalas is to put them on a clean, soft surface, such as a blanket or towel, gently tug them into the right shape with your hands and then cover with a damp (clean) towel. After a while, check on your (now damp) mandala, adjust the shape again if necessary and put the towel on top of it again. Leave for at least a couple of hours

(up to a day) and then remove the towel and let the mandala dry naturally. This is especially great for solid mandalas and those with a circular final round.

If the mandala has a border with sharp-edged curves, you could use pins (at the edges) to secure the mandala to the soft backing in the correct shape. Lightly spray with water, repeat if necessary and leave to dry.

If you're looking for a really quick blocking technique, you could use an iron. However, never use an iron for an acrylic (or acrylic blend) yarn. For all other yarns, check the label first.

Gently tug your work into the right shape and use the steam function of your iron to settle it. Then leave to dry naturally. Hold the iron about a centimetre above the mandala, and move the iron across the whole piece. Do not press the iron directly on to the mandala.

CROCHET REFRESHER COURSE

Even experienced crocheters need their memories jogged from time to time. Whether you're a relative beginner or have been crocheting for years, these pages provide a handy reference guide for how to do the most essential crochet stitches and key techniques.

Slip knot •

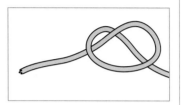

1. Make a yarn loop, as pictured.

2. Insert your crochet hook, as shown.

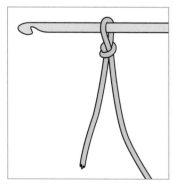

3. Gently pull on the short and long ends of yarn while holding the hook to create a slip knot.

Magic ring ℮

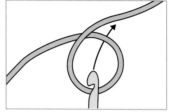

1. Start by making a loop in the yarn, as pictured. Insert the hook into the loop, following the direction of the arrow.

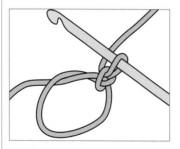

3. Make one chain stitch (or more, if directed by the pattern).

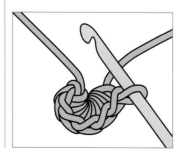

Chain stitch (ch) ○

2. Hook the working yarn (the long end) and pull it through the loop, as pictured.

4. Crochet the desired number of stitches into the centre of the loop.

5. Pull on the short yarn end to close the centre of the magic ring.

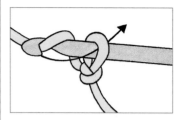

1. Make a slip knot as shown on the left. Wrap the yarn over the hook (or catch it with the hook) and pull it through the loop in the direction shown to make a new loop.

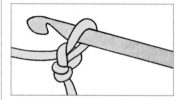

2. One chain stitch (ch) has now been made.

3. Repeat Steps 1–2 as required, moving your left hand every few stitches to hold the chain just below the hook. Tighten the slip knot by pulling on the short yarn tail.

Slip stitch (sl st) •

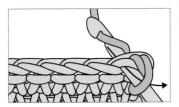

1. Insert the hook in the designated stitch, wrap the yarn over the hook and pull a new loop through both the work and the loop on the hook. One slip stitch (sl st) made.

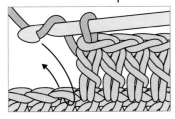

2. Repeat Step 1 in each stitch to the end to complete one row of slip stitches.

Double crochet (dc) +

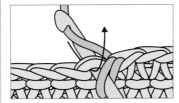

1. Insert the hook in the designated stitch, wrap the yarn over the hook and pull the new loop through this stitch only.

2. Wrap the yarn over the hook and then pull a loop through both loops on the hook.

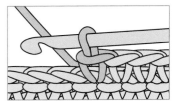

3. One loop remains on the hook. One double crochet stitch (dc) made. Repeat Steps 1–2 in each stitch to the end to complete one row of double crochet stitches.

Half treble crochet (htr) T

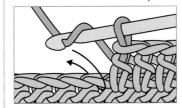

1. Wrap the yarn over the hook and then insert the hook in the designated stitch.

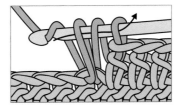

2. Pull a loop through this stitch. You now have three loops on the hook. Wrap the yarn over the hook again and pull it through all three loops on the hook.

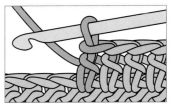

3. One loop remains on the hook. One half treble crochet stitch (htr) made. Repeat Steps 1–2 in each stitch to the end to complete one row of half treble crochet stitches.

Treble crochet (tr) T

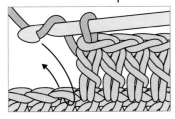

1. Wrap the yarn over the hook and then insert the hook in the designated stitch.

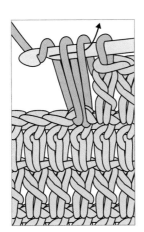

2. Pull a loop through this stitch to make three loops on the hook. Wrap the yarn over the hook again. Pull a new loop through the first two loops on the hook. Two loops remain on the hook. Wrap the yarn over the hook again. Pull a new loop through both loops on the hook.

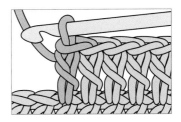

3. One loop remains on the hook. One treble crochet stitch (tr) made. Repeat Steps 1–2 in each stitch to the end to complete one row of treble crochet stitches.

22

Double treble crochet (dtr)

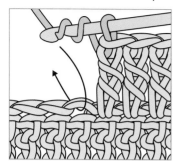

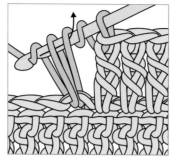

1. Wrap the yarn twice over the hook and then insert the hook in the designated stitch.

2. Pull a loop through this stitch. You now have four loops on the hook. Wrap the yarn over again and pull it through the first two loops.

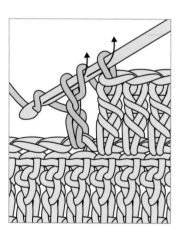

3. Three loops remain on the hook. Wrap the yarn over the hook and pull it through the first two loops.

4. Two loops remain on the hook. Wrap the yarn over again and pull it through the two remaining loops.

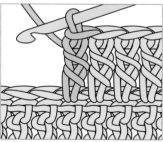

5. One loop remains on the hook. One double treble crochet stitch (dtr) made. Repeat Steps 1–4 in each stitch to the end to complete one row of double trebles.

'Post' Stitches

These are created by inserting the hook around the post of a stitch below, from the front or back, and are a great way to add texture to your crochet work: front post stitches are slightly raised and back post stitches slightly recede. The two examples shown here are the front post treble crochet (FPtr) and the back post treble crochet (BPtr), which are the most common, but most regular stitches can be worked as front or back post stitches. The only thing that sets them apart is where they are worked.

Front post treble crochet (FPtr)

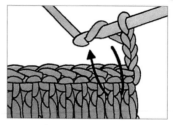

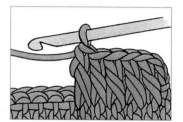

1. Wrap the yarn over the hook. Inserting the hook through the work from front to back, take it from right to left around the post of specified stitch below and then bring it through to the front again.

2. Complete the stitch in the usual way: yarn over (yo) and pull through, giving you three loops on the hook, [yo and pull through two loops on hook] twice. A ridge forms on the side of the work facing away from you.

Back post treble crochet (BPtr)

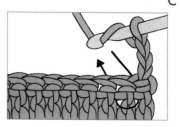

1. Wrap the yarn over the hook. Inserting the hook through the work from back to front, take it from right to left around the post of the specified stitch below and then take it through to the back again.

2. Complete the stitch in the usual way (see above). A ridge forms on the side of the work facing you.

Standing Stitches

A standing stitch (often called a st st) is a great way to start a round without using chains.

Standing double crochet (st dc)

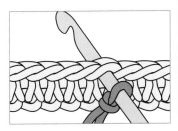

1. Make a slip knot on the hook and insert the hook in the indicated stitch or space.

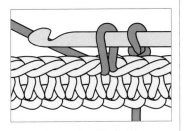

2. From here it's just like finishing a regular dc: yarn over, pull up a loop, yarn over and pull through both loops on the hook.

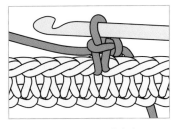

3. Your st dc will have a little bump on the back (the initial slip knot). If you wish, you can unravel this bump after completing the round; the st dc will stay secure.

Standing treble crochet (st tr) – method A

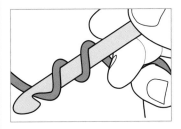

1. Wrap yarn around the hook twice. Secure these loops with a finger (this part can be a bit fiddly at first, but after a few times you will get the hang of it).

2. Insert the hook in the indicated stitch or space and pull up a loop.

3. From here it's like continuing making a regular tr: [yarn over and pull it through two loops] twice.

Standing treble crochet (st tr) – method B

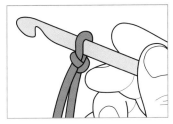

1. Make a slip knot on the hook.

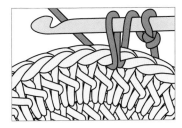

2. Yarn over and insert the hook in the indicated stitch or space. Pull up a loop.

3. From here it's like continuing making a regular tr: [yarn over and pull it through two loops] twice.

This method will leave a little bump on the back (the initial slip knot), but you can unravel this bump after completing the round. The st tr will stay secure.

Variations of the standing treble crochet

If you've mastered the standing treble crochet, it's easy to make variations. For instance:

Standing tr2tog

If your pattern calls for a tr2tog as the first stitch of a round, start by making a standing treble crochet, but don't finish it (just like you wouldn't finish a regular tr when working a tr2tog), but start working the second tr to finish the tr2tog.

Standing htr or standing dtr

For a standing htr, follow Steps 1–2 of the st tr (above) and then yo and pull through all three loops on the hook. If your pattern calls for a double treble (dtr) as the first stitch of a round, use the same technique as for the standing tr, but wrap the yarn around the hook three times (instead of two).

Working into One Loop Only

If the hook is inserted under just one loop at the top of a stitch, the empty loop creates a ridge on either the front or the back of the fabric. Throughout this book, 'front loop' means the loop nearest to you, at the top of the stitch, and 'back loop' means the farther loop, whether you are working a right-side or a wrong-side row.

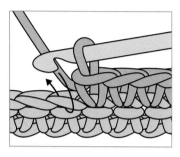

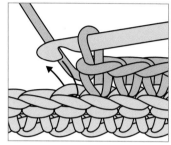

Front loop only (FL) ⌣

If the hook is inserted under the front loop only, the empty back loop will show as a ridge on the other side of the work.

Back loop only (BL) ⌢

If the hook is inserted under the back loop only, the empty front loop creates a ridge on the side of the work facing you. This example shows double crochet.

Working stitches together

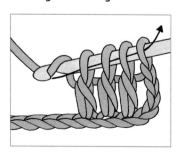

Several stitches may be joined together at the top to decrease the total number of stitches. This can be denoted in the pattern using the abbreviation 'tog' along with the type and number of stitches. For example, tr3tog describes 3 treble crochet stitches worked together.

To work a tr3tog (as shown on the left): work each of the stitches to be joined up to the last 'yo, pull through' that will complete it. One loop from each stitch will remain on the hook, plus the loop from the previous stitch. Yo once more and then pull a loop through all the loops on the hook to complete. Any number of any type of stitch can be worked together in a similar way.

Working into a chain space

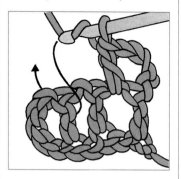

The hook is inserted into the space below one or more chains. Here, a treble crochet stitch is being worked into a one chain space (ch-1 sp).

Working several stitches in the same place

This technique is used to increase the total number of stitches. Increases may be worked at the edges of flat pieces, or at any point along a row. Two, three or more stitches may be worked into the same place to make a fan of stitches, often called a shell.

Joining Rounds

Joining with a slip stitch

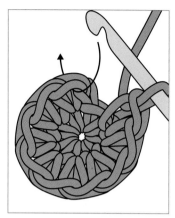

When you reach the end of the round, simply make a slip stitch into the very first stitch of the round, inserting the hook as shown here. The result is shown below.

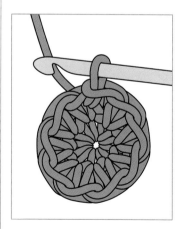

Joining with a needle

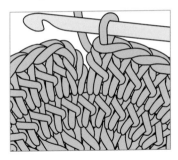

1. Complete the last stitch of the round. Cut the yarn, leaving a tail of about 10cm (4in).

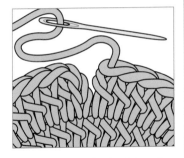

2. Remove the crochet hook from the last loop and draw the tail through the loop. Thread the tail on to a blunt yarn or tapestry needle.

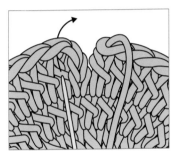

3. Insert the needle under both of the top V-shaped loops to the left of the first stitch (or starting chain). Draw the yarn all the way through.

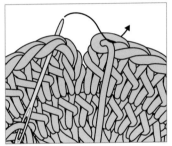

4. Insert the needle in between the top V-shaped loops, from front to back, of the last stitch you worked (at the end of the round).

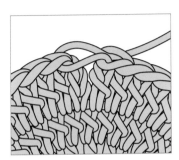

5. Pull the yarn through.

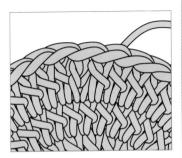

6. Adjust the tension until the join is seamless. Weave in the end.

Fastening Off and Weaving in Ends

It is very easy to fasten off yarn when you have finished a piece of crochet, but do not cut the yarn too close to the work because you need enough yarn to weave in the end. It is important to weave in yarn ends securely so that they do not unravel. Do this as neatly as possible so that the woven yarn does not show through on the front of the work.

Fastening off

To fasten off the yarn securely, work one chain, then cut the yarn at least 10cm (4in) away from the work and pull the tail through the loop on the hook, tightening it gently.

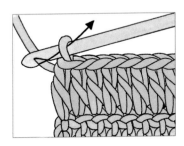

Weaving in yarn

To weave in a yarn end along the top or lower edge of a piece of crochet, start by threading the end into a blunt yarn or tapestry needle. Take the needle through several stitches on the wrong side of the crochet, working stitch by stitch. Trim the remaining yarn. When crocheting mandalas, try to weave your ends through the lower stitches as this will make the ends less visible.

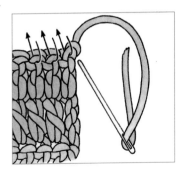

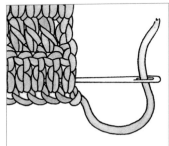

4

6

5

1

2

3

4

5

6

1

2

3

31 MANDALA SELECTOR

4

5

6

Oriental Lily (1), 76

Marvellous Myriad (2), 60

Delightful Doily (3), 100

Tulips from Amsterdam (4), 72

African Flower Love (5), 74

Rajasthan (6), 52

1

2

3

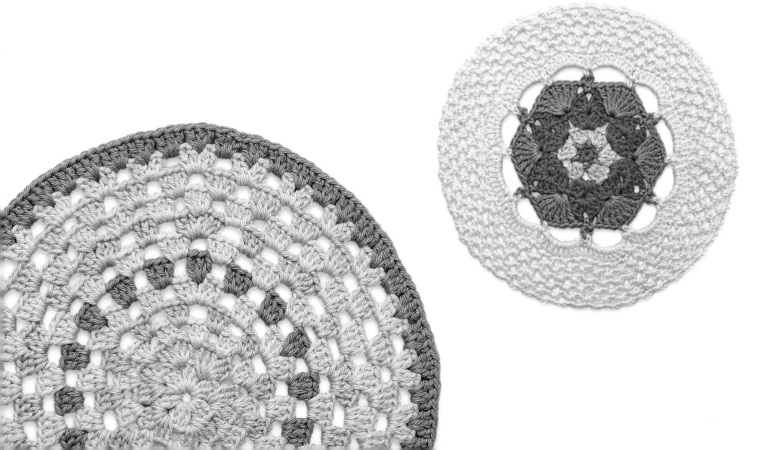

MANDALA PATTERNS

In this section you will find 30 of my favourite mandala patterns for you to try out. They range from the simplest designs, using only double crochet stitches, to more advanced patterns, with more complex stitches and added texture. Pages 16–17 offer lots of useful guidance, so do give them a read before you begin.

COURTLY CROWN

By using just the most basic of all stitches, you can create this beautiful piece. The humble double crochet stitch creates a sturdy yet refined texture. The elegant border is the crown on this mandala.

Hook size: 3.5mm
Diameter: 18cm (7in)

Note:
The basic number of sts of this mandala is 6. This means that in every round you will increase the number of sts by 6.

Chart Key
○ ch
• sl st
+ dc
Ŧ tr
◀ start of round

To start (colour A): Make a magic ring or ch 4 and sl st in first ch to form a ring.

Round 1: 6 dc in ring. Join.

Round 2: *2 dc in each st. Join. (Increase every st.)

Round 3: *Dc in first st, 2 dc in next st; rep from * five more times. Join. (Increase every other st.)

Round 4: *Dc in 2 sts, 2 dc in next st; rep from * five more times. Join. (Increase every 3rd st.)

Round 5: *Dc in 3 sts, 2 dc in next st; rep from * five more times. Join. (Increase every 4th st.)

Round 6 (colour B): *Dc in 4 sts, 2 dc in next st; rep from * five more times. Join. (Increase every 5th st.)

Round 7 (colour C): *Dc in 5 sts, 2 dc in next st; rep from * five more times. Join. (Increase every 6th st.)

Round 8: *Dc in 6 sts, 2 dc in next st; rep from * five more times. Join. (Increase every 7th st.)

Round 9: *Dc in 7 sts, 2 dc in next st; rep from * five more times. Join. (Increase every 8th st.)

Round 10: *Dc in 8 sts, 2 dc in next st; rep from * five more times. Join. (Increase every 9th st.)

Round 11 (colour B): *Dc in 9 sts, 2 dc in next st; rep from * five more times. Join. (Increase every 10th st.)

Round 12 (colour D): *Dc in 10 sts, 2 dc in next st; rep from * five more times. Join. (Increase every 11th st.)

Round 13: *Dc in 11 sts, 2 dc in next st; rep from * five more times. Join. (Increase every 12th st.)

Round 14: *Dc in 12 sts, 2 dc in next st; rep from * five more times. Join. (Increase every 13th st.)

Round 15: *Dc in 13 sts, 2 dc in next st; rep from * five more times. Join. (Increase every 14th st.)

Round 16 (colour B): *Dc in 14 sts, 2 dc in next st; rep from * five more times. Join. (Increase every 15th st.)

Round 17 (colour A): *Dc in 15 sts, 2 dc in next st; rep from * five more times. Join. (Increase every 16th st.)

Round 18: *Dc in 16 sts, 2 dc in next st; rep from * five more times. Join. (Increase every 17th st.)

Round 19: *Dc in 17 sts, 2 dc in next st; rep from * five more times. Join. (Increase every 18th st.)

Round 20: *Dc in 18 sts, 2 dc in next st; rep from * five more times. Join. (Increase every 19th st.)

Round 21 (colour B): Dc in each st. Join.

To make a really smooth circle there are no increases in the last round of dc sts. You might want to switch to a slightly larger hook to prevent the mandala from 'cupping' (see page 19).

Round 22: *Dc in st, skip next 2 dc, 5 tr in next st, skip next 2 dc; rep from * 19 more times. Join.

Fasten off. Weave in ends.

GO WITH THE FLOW

This eyecatcher is created by working with two strands of yarn simultaneously, which makes the colours seem to flow. This simple technique gives your mandala just that little something extra.

Hook size: 6mm
Diameter: 25cm (9¾in)

Notes:

• The basic number of sts of this mandala is 10. This means that in every round you will increase the number of sts by 10.

• For this mandala two strands of yarn have been held together throughout. The colours used vary per round in order to make a personalised mandala.

To start: Make a magic ring or ch 4 and sl st in first ch to form a ring.

Round 1: 10 htr in ring. Join.

Round 2: 2 htr in each st. Join. (Increase every st.)

Round 3: *Htr in next st, 2 htr in next st; rep from * nine more times. Join. (Increase every other st.)

Round 4: *Htr in 2 sts, 2 htr in next st; rep from * nine more times. Join. (Increase every 3rd st.)

Round 5: *Htr in 3 sts, 2 htr in next st; rep from * nine more times. Join. (Increase every 4th st.)

Round 6: *Htr in 4 sts, 2 htr in next st; rep from * nine more times. Join. (Increase every 5th st.)

Round 7: *Htr in 5 sts, 2 htr in next st; rep from * nine more times. Join. (Increase every 6th st.)

Round 8: *Htr in 6 sts, 2 htr in next st; rep from * nine more times. Join. (Increase every 7th st.)

Round 9: *Htr in 7 sts, 2 htr in next st; rep from * nine more times. Join. (Increase every 8th st.)

Round 10: *Htr in 8 sts, 2 htr in next st; rep from * nine more times. Join. (Increase every 9th st.)

Round 11: *Htr in 9 sts, 2 htr in next st; rep from * nine more times. Join. (Increase every 10th st.)

Round 12: *Htr in 10 sts, 2 htr in next st; rep from * nine more times. Join. (Increase every 11th st.)

Fasten off. Weave in ends.

Chart Key
◠ ch
• sl st
T htr
◄ start of round

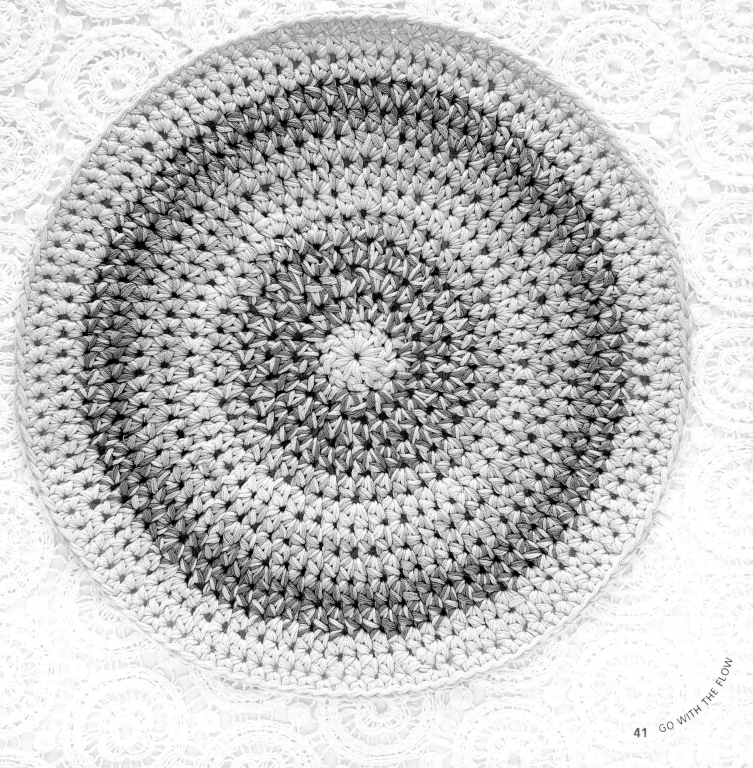

HANDSOME HOOPS

The treble crochet is a favourite stitch for many crocheters and it's just perfect to create this impeccable circle. Lovely pastels turn this simple mandala into a thing of beauty. Add a border of your choice from pages 102–105 if desired.

Hook size: 3mm
Diameter: 19.5cm (7¾in)

Note:
The basic number of sts of this mandala is 12. This means that in every round you will increase the number of sts by 12.

To start (colour A): Make a magic ring or ch 4 and sl st in first ch to form a ring.

Round 1: 12 tr in ring. Join.

Round 2: 2 tr in each st. Join. (Increase every st.)

Round 3: *Tr in next st, 2 tr in next st; rep from * 11 more times. Join. (Increase every other st.)

Round 4: *Tr in 2 sts, 2 tr in next st; rep from * 11 more times. Join. (Increase every 3rd st.)

Round 5 (colour B): *Tr in 3 sts, 2 tr in next st; rep from * 11 more times. Join. (Increase every 4th st.)

Round 6 (colour C): *Tr in 4 sts, 2 tr in next st; rep from * 11 more times. Join. (Increase every 5th st.)

Round 7: *Tr in 5 sts, 2 tr in next st; rep from * 11 more times. Join. (Increase every 6th st.)

Round 8: *Tr in 6 sts, 2 tr in next st; rep from * 11 more times. Join. (Increase every 7th st.)

Round 9 (colour B): *Tr in 7 sts, 2 tr in next st; rep from * 11 more times. Join. (Increase every 8th st.)

Round 10 (colour D): *Tr in 8 sts, 2 tr in next st; rep from * 11 more times. Join. (Increase every 9th st.)

Round 11: *Tr in 9 sts, 2 tr in next st; rep from * 11 more times. Join. (Increase every 10th st.)

Round 12 (colour B): *Tr in 10 sts, 2 tr in next st; rep from * 11 more times. Join. (Increase every 11th st.)

Fasten off. Weave in ends.

Chart Key
- ◠ ch
- • sl st
- ╪ tr
- ◄ start of round

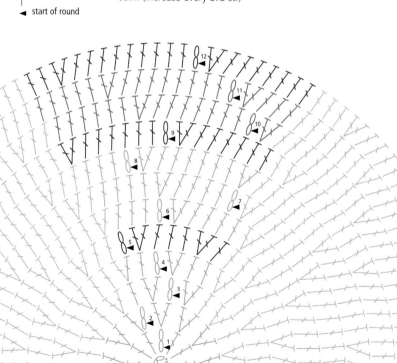

GRANNY CIRCLE

Who doesn't love the good old Granny Square? Its round equivalent is every bit as lovable and versatile. Make it in all your favourite colours!

Hook size: 3mm
Diameter: 20.5cm (8in)

Chart Key
○ ch
• sl st
⊤ tr
◄ start of round

To start (colour A): Make a magic ring or ch 6 and sl st in first ch to form a ring.

Round 1: *3 tr in ring, ch 1; rep from * five more times. Join.

Round 2 (colour B): *[3 tr, ch 1, 3 tr] in ch-1 sp, ch 1; rep from * five more times. Join.

Round 3 (colour C): *3 tr in ch-1 sp, ch 1; rep from * 11 more times. Join.

Round 4 (colour D): *3 tr in ch-1 sp, ch 3, 3 tr in next ch-1 sp, ch 2; rep from * five more times. Join.

Round 5 (colour E): *[3 tr, ch 1, 3 tr] in ch-3 sp, ch 2, 3 tr in ch-2 sp, ch 2; rep from * five more times. Join.

Round 6 (colour F): *3 tr in ch-1 sp, ch 2, [3 tr in ch-2 sp, ch 2] twice; rep from * five more times. Join.

Round 7 (colour G): *4 tr in ch-2 sp, ch 2; rep from * 17 more times. Join.

Round 8 (colour H): *3 tr in ch-2 sp, ch 2, [3 tr, ch 1, 3 tr] in next ch-2 sp, ch 2; rep from * eight more times. Join.

Round 9 (colour I): *4 tr in ch-1 sp, ch 1, [4 tr in ch-2 sp, ch 1] twice; rep from * eight more times. Join.

Round 10 (colour G): *4 tr in ch-1 sp, ch 2; rep from * 26 more times. Join.

Round 11 (colour D): *[2 tr, ch 1, 2 tr] in ch-2 sp, ch 2; rep from * 26 more times. Join.

Round 12 (colour E): *3 tr in ch-2 sp, 3 tr in ch-1 sp; rep from * 26 more times. Join.

Fasten off. Weave in ends.

PEBBLE IN THE POND

A wee twist on a simple pattern changes the look of this treble crochet mandala. By just working in the back loops, an intriguing texture will emerge.

Hook size: 3mm
Diameter: 23cm (9in)

Chart Key
○ ch
• sl st
╈ tr
╈ BLtr
⋏ BLdc
◄ start of round

To start (colour A): Make a magic ring or ch 4 and sl st in first ch to form a ring.

Round 1: 12 tr in ring. Join.

Round 2 (colour B): 2 BLtr in each st. Join. (Increase every st.)

Round 3 (colour C): *BLtr in next st, 2 BLtr in next st; rep from * 11 more times. Join. (Increase every other st.)

Round 4 (colour D): At this point we will repeat Round 3 (increasing every other st) to prevent the mandala from cupping

(see page 19). *BLtr in next st, 2 BLtr in next st; rep from * 17 more times. Join.

Round 5 (colour A): *BLtr in 2 sts, 2 BLtr in next st; rep from * 17 more times. Join. (Increase every 3rd st.)

Round 6 (colour B): *BLtr in 3 sts, 2 BLtr in next st; rep from * 17 more times. Join. (Increase every 4th st.)

Round 7 (colour C): *BLtr in 4 sts, 2 BLtr in next st; rep from * 17 more times. Join. (Increase every 5th st.)

Round 8 (colour D): *BLtr in 5 sts, 2 BLtr in next st; rep from * 17 more times. Join. (Increase every 6th st.)

Round 9 (colour A): *BLtr in 6 sts, 2 BLtr in next st; rep from * 17 more times. Join. (Increase every 7th st.)

Round 10 (colour B): *BLtr in 7 sts, 2 BLtr in next st; rep from * 17 more times. Join. (Increase every 8th st.)

Round 11 (colour C): *BLtr in 8 sts, 2 BLtr in next st; rep from * 17 more times. Join. (Increase every 9th st.)

Round 12 (colour D): *BLtr in 9 sts, 2 BLtr in next st; rep from * 17 more times. Join. (Increase every 10th st.)

Round 13: BLdc in each st. Join.

Fasten off. Weave in ends.

PRETTY PIECES

Simple, yet elegant – that's the Pretty Pieces mandala in a nutshell. It doesn't need a lot of counting, which makes it a relaxing pattern to make. Try it with lots of different colours!

Hook size: 3mm
Diameter: 21.5cm
(8½in)

Note:
Since this is a lacy pattern, you can place the first st of each round on top of the first st of the previous round.

To start (colour A): Make a magic ring or ch 7 and sl st in first ch to form a ring.

Round 1: 10 dc in ring. Join.

Round 2 (colour B): *Tr in next st, ch 3; rep from * nine more times. Join.

Round 3: *3 tr in ch-3 sp, ch 2; rep from * nine more times. Join.

Round 4: *Tr in first tr, 2 tr in next st, tr in next st, ch 2; rep from * nine more times. Join.

Round 5: *Tr in first tr, 2 tr in next st, tr in next 2 sts, ch 2; rep from * nine more times. Join.

Round 6: *Tr in first tr, [2 tr in next st, tr in next st] twice, ch 2; rep from * nine more times. Join.

Round 7: *Tr in first tr, 2 tr in next st, tr in next 3 sts, 2 tr in next st, tr in next st, ch 2; rep from * nine more times. Join.

Round 8: *Tr in first tr, 2 tr in next st, tr in next 5 sts, 2 tr in next st, tr in next st, ch 2; rep from * nine more times. Join.

Round 9: *Tr in 5 sts, 2 tr in next st, tr in next 5 sts, ch 2; rep from * nine more times. Join.

Round 10: *Tr in first tr, 2 tr in next st, tr in next 10 sts, ch 2; rep from * nine more times. Join.

Round 11: *Tr in 11 sts, 2 tr in next st, tr in next st, ch 2; rep from * nine more times. Join.

Round 12 (colour A): *Tr in 14 sts, 2 tr in ch-2 sp; rep from * nine more times. Join.

Round 13: Crab st in each st. Join.

Fasten off. Weave in ends.

Chart Key
⌒ ch
• sl st
+ dc
T tr
◀ start of round

Special Stitch (see p.125)
⨙ crab st

INSTRUCTIONS

FLIRTY FIFTIES

Yes, the Fifties are back with this retro mandala! The popcorn stitches in the centre of this piece and the adorable wavy border are really eye-catching.

Hook size: 3mm
Diameter: 25cm
(9¾in)

To start (colour A): Make a magic ring or ch 8 and sl st in first ch to form a ring.

Round 1: *Tr3tog in ring, ch 3; rep from * seven more times. Join.

Round 2 (colour B): *Pc in ch-3 sp, ch 5; rep from * seven more times. Join.

Round 3 (colour A): *3 tr in ch-3 sp of Round 1 (to the right of pc in same sp), ch 4, skip pc; rep from * seven more times. Join.

Round 4: *Tr in 3 sts, 3 tr in ch-4 sp; rep from * seven more times. Join.

Round 5: *Tr in 2 sts, 2 tr in next st; rep from * 15 more times. Join.

Round 6: *Tr in 3 sts, 2 tr in next st; rep from * 15 more times. Join.

Round 7: *Tr2tog in tr, ch 2, skip next tr; rep from * 39 more times. Join.

Round 8 (colour C): *Tr3tog in ch-2 sp, ch 2; rep from * 39 more times. Join.

Round 9 (colour A): *Tr3tog in ch-2 sp, ch 3; rep from * 39 more times. Join.

Round 10 (colour D): *Tr4tog in ch-3 sp, ch 4; rep from * 39 more times. Join.

Round 11 (colour A): *4 tr in ch-4 sp, tr in tr4tog cluster; rep from * 39 more times. Join.

Round 12: *9 tr in tr placed on top of tr4tog cluster (shell made), skip next 4 tr, dc in next tr, skip next 4 tr; rep from * 19 more times. Join.

Round 13: *Dc in 3rd tr of shell, dc in next 4 sts, ch 7; rep from * 19 more times. Join.

Round 14 (colour C): *Dc in 2nd dc, dc in next 2 sts, skip next dc, 9 tr in ch-7 sp; rep from * 19 more times. Join.

Fasten off. Weave in ends.

Chart Key
- ◯ ch
- • sl st
- ⋔ tr3tog
- ⊤ tr
- ⬦ tr2tog
- ⋔ tr4tog
- ◄ start of round

Special Stitch (see p.125)
- ⬭ pc = 5 tr popcorn

RAJASTHAN

The inspiration for this mandala came from the intricate window screens in the palaces of Rajasthan, India. It's almost magical to see the circle in the centre transform into a star and then into a hexagon.

Hook size: 3mm
Diameter: 17cm (6¾in)

To start (colour A): Make a magic ring or ch 4 and sl st in first ch to form a ring.

Round 1: 6 dc in ring. Join.

Round 2 (colour B): *Sl st in dc, ch 3; rep from * five more times. Join.

Round 3 (colour C): *3 tr in ch-3 sp, ch 3; rep from * five more times. Join.

Round 4 (colour A): *[3 tr, ch 2, 3 tr] in ch-3 sp; rep from * five more times. Join.

Round 5: *Dc in sp between [3 tr, ch 2, 3 tr] clusters, [3 tr, ch 3, 3 tr] in ch-2 sp; rep from * five more times. Join.

Round 6 (colour B): *Dc in ch-3 sp, picot-4, ch 1, skip 3 tr, 7 dtr in dc, ch 1, skip 3 tr; rep from * five more times. Join.

Round 7 (colour D): *Dc in picot, ch 7, skip 3 dtr, dc in 4th dtr, skip 3 dtr, ch 7; rep from * five more times. Join.

Round 8: *8 tr in ch-7 sp, tr in dc; rep from * 11 more times. Join.

Round 9: *Dc in tr, ch 3, skip next tr; rep from * 53 more times. Join.

Round 10: *Dc in ch-3 sp, ch 3; rep from * 53 more times. Join.

Round 11: *Dc in ch-3 sp, ch 3; rep from * 53 more times. Join.

Round 12: *Dc in ch-3 sp, ch 3; rep from * 53 more times. Join.

Round 13: *Dc in ch-3 sp, ch 3; rep from * 53 more times. Join.

Fasten off. Weave in ends.

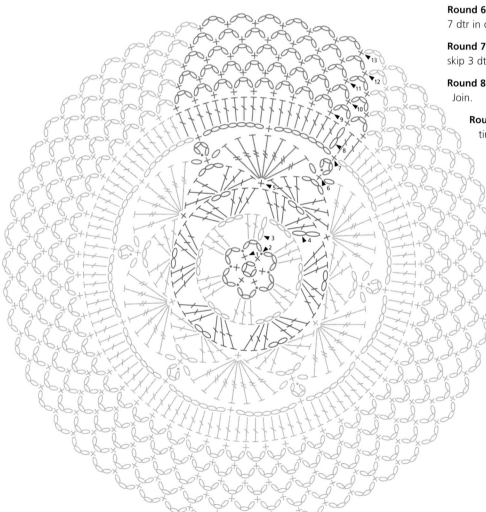

Chart Key

- ◯ ch
- • sl st
- + dc
- ⊤ tr
- ⊤⧸ dtr
- ◀ start of round

Special Stitch (see p.125)

- 🪢 picot-4

ICE CREAM

This mandala certainly reminds me of my favourite dessert. Create your own variation on this pattern by adding a border from pages 102–105. This mandala would work well in bold, bright colours, too.

Hook size: 3mm
Diameter: 22.5cm
(8¾in)

Note:
To make this mandala, you first make seven separate triangles, then stitch or crochet them together to form a circle. When the mandala is pieced together, you crochet the 13th round.

To start: Ch 3.

Row 1: Tr in first ch from hook. Turn. (2 tr.)

Row 2: 2 tr in each st. Turn.

Row 3: 2 tr in first st, tr in next 2 sts, 2 tr in next st. Turn.

Row 4: 2 tr in first st, tr in next 4 sts, 2 tr in next st. Turn.

Row 5: 2 tr in first st, tr in next 6 sts, 2 tr in next st. Turn.

Row 6: 2 tr in first st, tr in next 8 sts, 2 tr in next st. Turn.

Row 7: 2 tr in first st, tr in next 10 sts, 2 tr in next st. Turn.

Row 8: 2 tr in first st, tr in next 12 sts, 2 tr in next st. Turn.

Row 9: 2 tr in first st, tr in next 14 sts, 2 tr in next st. Turn.

Row 10: 2 tr in first st, tr in next 16 sts, 2 tr in next st. Turn.

Row 11: 2 tr in first st, tr in next 18 sts, 2 tr in next st. Turn.

Row 12: 2 tr in first st, tr in next 20 sts, 2 tr in next st. Turn.

Complete 7 triangles, one in each colour A–G.

Assembling:

To sew the mandala together: Using a matching yarn and blunt needle and working from the back of the triangles, whipstitch through the outer loops.

To crochet the mandala together: Using a matching yarn and holding the triangles together with right sides facing, slip stitch through the outer loops.

Edge: The final round consists of all seven colours used for the triangles. You'll change colour on the go and make 26 treble crochet stitches with each colour. Start with colour A and make a standing treble in the second-to-last tr of a triangle in a contrasting colour. (The reason you start here, instead of in the middle of the triangle, is to ensure a smooth join in the same colour when you close the round.) Then work the round as follows:

Round 13: 2 tr in next tr, tr in next 11 sts, 2 tr in next st, change colour, *tr in next 11 sts, 2 tr in next st, tr in next 11 sts, 2 tr in next st, change colour; rep from * five more times, rejoin colour A, tr in next 10 sts. Join.

Fasten off. Weave in ends.

Chart Key
◦ ch
⊤ tr
◄ start of row

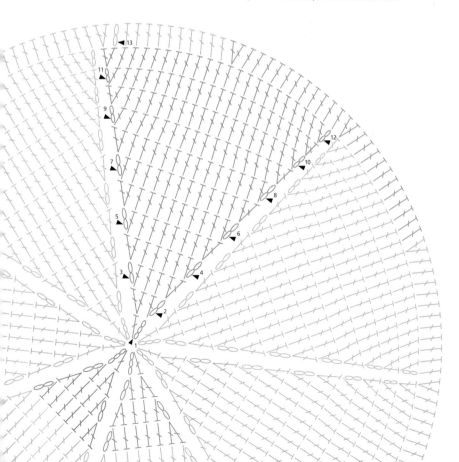

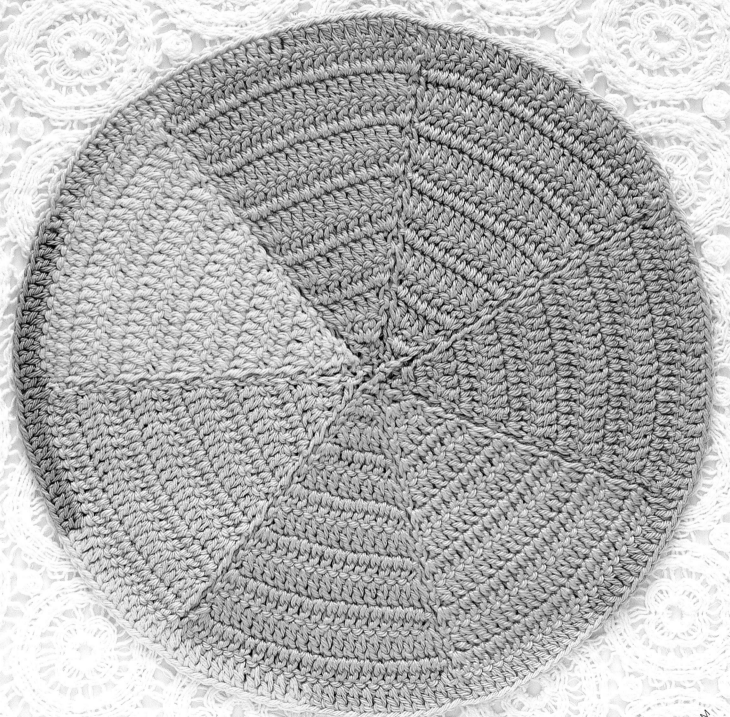

STARRY, STARRY NIGHT

This mandala is a true classic. The ripple stitches create a stunning star pattern, while the repeating rounds in white have a calming effect.

Hook size: 3mm
Diameter: 27.5cm
(10¾in)

Chart Key
⌒ ch
• sl st
† tr
◄ start of round

To start (colour A): Make a magic ring or ch 4 and sl st in first ch to form a ring.

Round 1: 12 tr in ring. Join.

Round 2: *Tr in tr, ch 2; rep from * 11 more times. Join.

Round 3 (colour B): *[Tr, ch 2, tr] in tr; rep from * 11 more times. Join.

Round 4: *[2 tr, ch 2, 2 tr] in ch-2 sp (shell made); rep from * 11 more times. Join.

Round 5 (colour A): *Tr in 2nd tr of shell, [2 tr, ch 2, 2 tr] in ch-2 sp, tr in next st (shell made), skip next 2 tr; rep from * 11 more times. Join.

Round 6 (colour C): *Tr in 2nd tr of shell, tr in next st, [2 tr, ch 2, 2 tr] in ch-2 sp, tr in next 2 sts (shell made), skip next 2 tr; rep from * 11 more times. Join.

Round 7: *Tr in 2nd tr of shell, tr in next 2 sts, [2 tr, ch 2, 2 tr] in ch-2 sp, tr in next 3 sts (shell made), skip next 2 tr; rep from * 11 more times. Join.

Round 8 (colour A): *Tr in 2nd tr of shell, tr in next 3 sts, [tr, ch 2, tr] in ch-2 sp, tr in next 4 sts (shell made), skip next 2 tr; rep from * 11 more times. Join.

Round 9 (colour D): *Tr in 2nd tr of shell, tr in next 3 sts, [2 tr, ch 2, 2 tr] in ch-2 sp, tr in next 4 sts (shell made), skip next 2 tr; rep from * 11 more times. Join.

Round 10: *Tr in 2nd tr of shell, tr in next 4 sts, [2 tr, ch 2, 2 tr] in ch-2 sp, tr in next 5 sts (shell made), skip next 2 tr; rep from * 11 more times. Join.

Round 11 (colour A): *Tr in 2nd tr of shell, tr in next 5 sts, [tr, ch 2, tr] in ch-2 sp, tr in next 6 sts, skip next 2 tr; rep from * 11 more times. Join.

Round 12 (colour E): *Tr in 2nd tr of shell, tr in next 5 sts, [2 tr, ch 2, 2 tr] in ch-2 sp, tr in next 6 sts, skip next 2 tr; rep from * 11 more times. Join.

Round 13: *Tr in 2nd tr of shell, tr in next 6 sts, [2 tr, ch 2, 2 tr] in ch-2 sp, tr in next 7 sts, skip next 2 tr; rep from * 11 more times. Join.

Fasten off. Weave in ends.

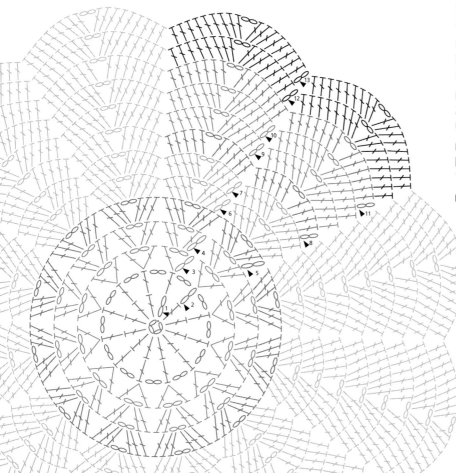

LOVELY LACE

Who says mandalas need to have a dense texture? This whimsical design is both breezy and very elegant. The gaps make it a fairly quick pattern to make, too.

Hook size: 3mm
Diameter: 19.5cm (7¾in)

To start (colour A): Make a magic ring or ch 8 and sl st in first ch to form a ring.

Round 1: *Puff in ring, ch 2; rep from * nine more times. Join.

Round 2 (colour B): *[Puff, ch 1, puff, ch 2] in ch-2 sp; rep from * nine more times. Join.

Round 3 (colour A): *Dc in ch-1 sp, ch 2, dc in ch-2 sp, ch 2; rep from * nine more times. Join.

Round 4: *2 dc in ch-2 sp, ch 1; rep from * 19 more times. Join.

Round 5: *Dc in ch-1 sp, ch 3; rep from * 19 more times. Join.

Round 6 (colour B): *3 tr in ch-3 sp, ch 1; rep from * 19 more times. Join.

Round 7 (colour A): *Dc in ch-1 sp, ch 3, dc in next ch-1 sp, ch 7; rep from * nine more times. Join.

Round 8: *Dc in ch-3 sp, 9 tr in ch-7 sp; rep from * nine more times. Join.

Round 9 (colour B): *Tr in 5th tr of shell, ch 13, skip next 9 sts; rep from * nine more times. Join.

Round 10: *Dc in tr, 15 tr in ch-1 sp; rep from * nine more times. Join.

Round 11 (colour A): *Tr in 8th tr of shell, ch 15, skip next 15 sts; rep from * nine more times. Join.

Round 12: *Dc in tr, 17 tr in ch-15 sp; rep from * nine more times. Join.

Fasten off. Weave in ends.

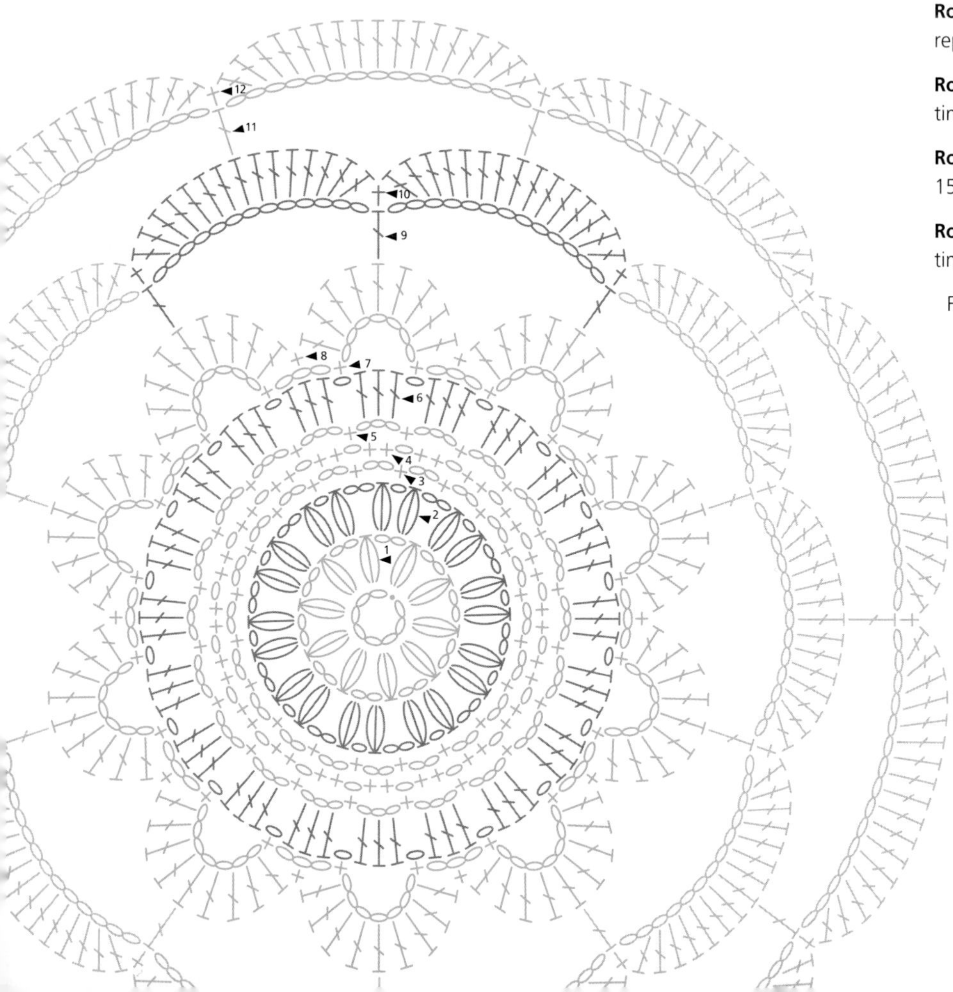

Chart Key
- ⌒ ch
- • sl st
- + dc
- † tr
- ◄ start of round

Special Stitch (see p.125)
- puff = puff stitch

MARVELLOUS MYRIAD

Oh dear, this is a big one – and I love it big time! I've chosen bright colours for this mandala, but it would look incredible in soft pastels, as well.

Hook size: 3mm
Diameter: 37.5cm
(14¾in)

To start (colour A): Make a magic ring or ch 5 and sl st in first ch to form a ring.

Round 1: 16 tr in ring. Join.

Round 2: 2 tr in each tr. Join. (32 tr.)

Round 3: *Tr in first st, 2 tr in next st; rep from * 15 more times. Join. (48 tr.)

Round 4 (colour B): *[Tr, ch 2, tr] in first st, skip 2 tr; rep from * 15 more times. Join.

Round 5 (colour C): *[2 tr, ch 2, 2 tr] in ch-2 sp; rep from * 15 more times. Join.

Round 6: *5 tr in ch-2 sp, ch 1; rep from * 15 more times. Join.

Round 7 (colour D): *Dc in ch-1 sp, ch 6; rep from * 15 more times. Join.

Round 8 (colour A): *5 tr in ch-6 sp, ch 1; rep from * 15 more times. Join.

Round 9: *Dc in 5 tr, dc in ch-1 sp; rep from * 15 more times. Join.

Round 10 (colour B): *[Tr, ch 3, tr] in dc (work first tr in dc worked in ch-1 sp of Round 8), skip 2 dc; rep from * 31 more times. Join.

Round 11 (colour E): *[Tr, ch 4, tr] in ch-3 sp; rep from * 31 more times. Join.

Round 12: *[2 tr, ch 2, 2 tr] in ch-4 sp; rep from * 31 more times. Join.

Round 13 (colour D): *[2 tr, ch 3, 2 tr] in ch-2 sp; rep from * 31 more times. Join.

Round 14 (colour E): *5 tr in ch-3 sp, ch 1; rep from * 31 more times. Join.

Round 15 (colour F): *Dc in ch-1 sp, ch 6; rep from * 31 more times. Join.

Round 16 (colour A): *6 tr in ch-6 sp, ch 1; rep from * 31 more times. Join.

Round 17 (colour G): *Dc in ch-1 sp, ch 7; rep from * 31 more times. Join.

Round 18 (colour E): *7 tr in ch-7 sp, ch 1; rep from * 31 more times. Join.

Round 19: *Dc in 7 tr, dc in ch-1 sp; rep from * 31 more times. Join.

Round 20: *[Tr, ch 2, tr] in dc (work first tr in dc worked in ch-1 sp of Round 18), skip 3 dc; rep from * 63 more times. Join.

Round 21: *[Tr, ch 3, tr] in ch-2 sp; rep from * 63 more times. Join.

Round 22: *[Tr, ch 3, tr] in ch-2 sp; rep from * 63 more times. Join.

Round 23: *[Tr, ch 4, tr] in ch-2 sp; rep from * 63 more times. Join.

Round 24: *[Tr, ch 4, tr] in ch-2 sp; rep from * 63 more times. Join.

Fasten off. Weave in ends.

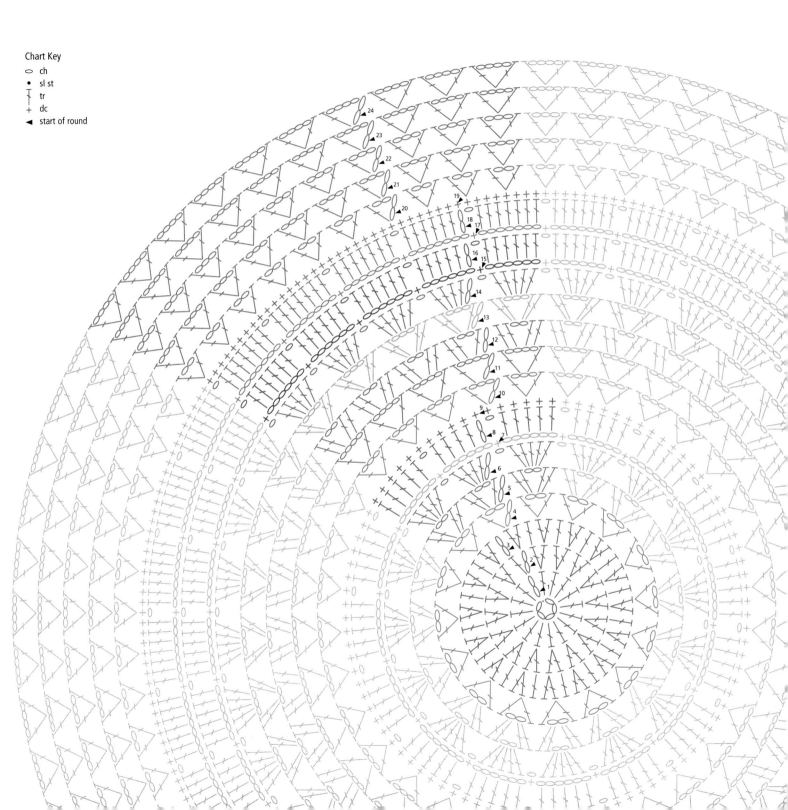

Chart Key
○ ch
• sl st
┬ tr
+ dc
◄ start of round

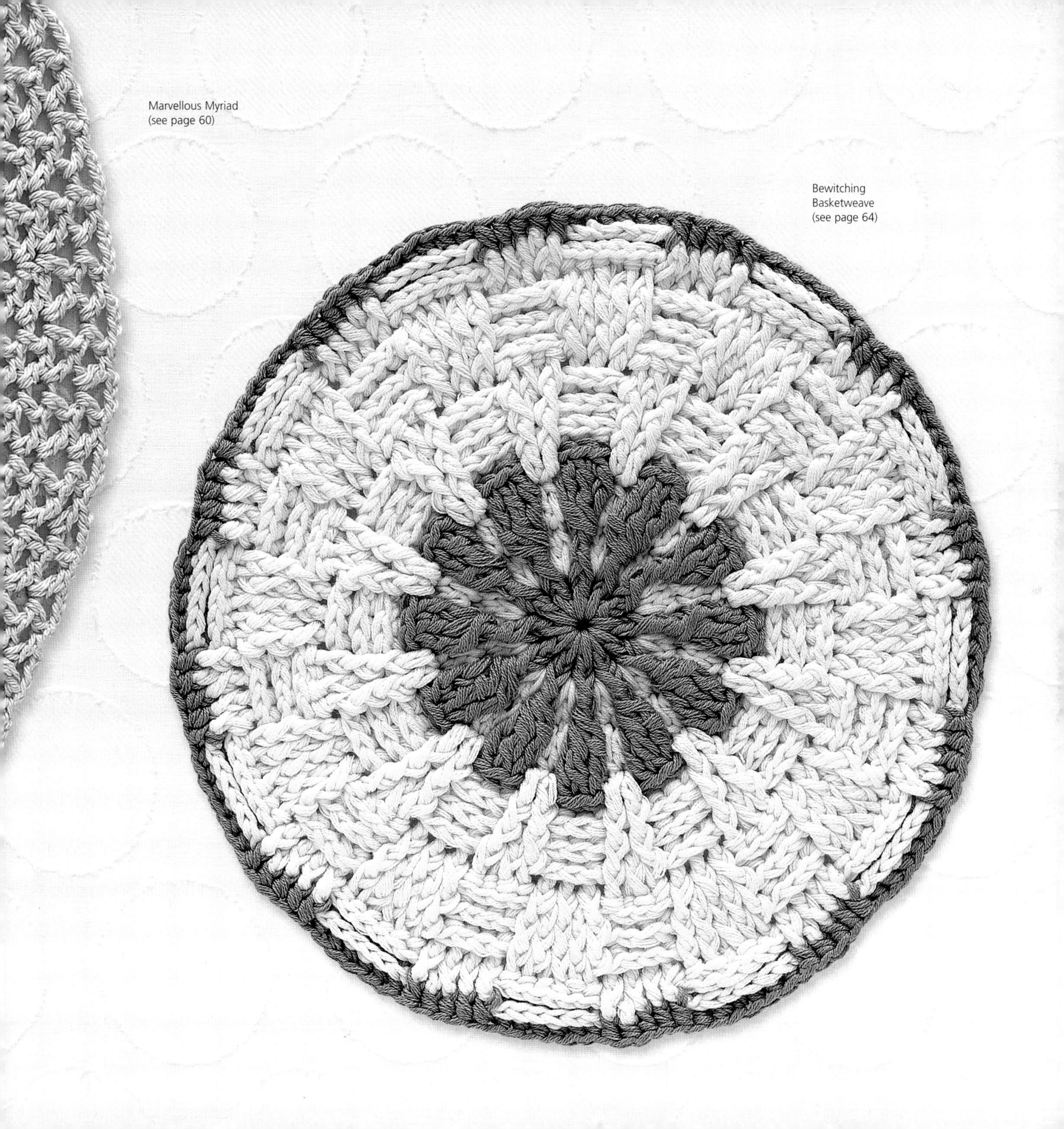

Marvellous Myriad
(see page 60)

Bewitching
Basketweave
(see page 64)

BEWITCHING BASKETWEAVE

The basketweave stitch is one of the most fascinating techniques and it's intriguing to see the pattern emerge. The chart might look a bit challenging at first glance, but with the help of the written pattern, it should pose no problem.

Hook size: 3.5mm

Diameter: 18.5cm (7¼in)

Note:
Additional colours have been used in this chart for added clarity.

To start (colour A): Make a magic ring or ch 5 and sl st in first ch to form a ring.

Round 1: *Tr in ring, ch 1; rep from * 11 more times. Join.

Round 2 (colour B): *Tr in tr, 2 tr in ch-1 sp; rep from * 11 more times. Join.

Round 3 (colour A): Start this round in the first of the 2 tr worked in ch-1 sp of Round 2. *BLdc in 3 tr, FPdtr in tr of Round 1; rep from * 11 more times. Join.

Round 4 (colour B): *2 BLtr in dtr, FLtr in next 2 tr of Round 2; rep from * 11 more times. Join.

Round 5 (colour A): Start this round in the first of the 2 FLtr of Round 4. *BLdc in 2 sts, 3 FPdtr in dtr of Round 3; rep from * 11 more times. Join.

Round 6 (colour B): This round is worked completely into the stitches of Round 4. Start this round in the first of the 2 tr of Round 4 between groups of 3 dtr. *FLtr in 2 tr, (work behind 3 dtr of Round 5): BLtr in tr, 2 BLtr in next st; rep from * 11 more times. Join.

Round 7: Start this round in the first of 2 FLtr of Round 6. *FPtr in next 2 tr, BPtr in next 3 sts; rep from * 11 more times. Join.

Round 8: Start this round in the first FPtr of any FPtr group of Round 7. *FPtr in first st, [tr, FPtr] in next st, BPtr in next 3 sts; rep from * 11 more times. Join.

Round 9: Start this round in the first FPtr of any FPtr group of Round 8. (Be careful not to miss the tr worked between the FPtr, which might be slightly hidden.) *FPtr in first st, [tr, FPtr] in next st, FPtr in next st, BPtr in next 3 sts; rep from * 11 more times. Join.

Round 10: Start this round in the first BPtr of any BPtr group of Round 9. *FPtr in first st, [tr, FPtr] in next 2 sts, BPtr in next 4 sts; rep from * 11 more times. Join.

Round 11: Start this round in the first FPtr of any FPtr group of Round 10. *FPtr in next 5 sts, BPtr in next 4 sts; rep from * 11 more times. Join.

Round 12: Start this round in the first FPtr of any FPtr group of Round 11. *FPtr in 2 sts, [tr, FPtr] in next st, FPtr in next 2 sts, BPtr in next 4 sts; rep from * 11 times. Join.

Round 13: Start this round in the first BPtr of any BPtr group of Round 12. *FPtr in first st, [tr, FPtr] in next st, FPtr in next 2 sts, BPtr in next 6 sts; rep from * 11 more times. Join.

Round 14 (colour A): Start this round in the first FPtr of any FPtr group of Round 13. *FPhtr in 5 sts, BPhtr in next 6 sts; rep from * 11 more times. Join.

Fasten off. Weave in ends.

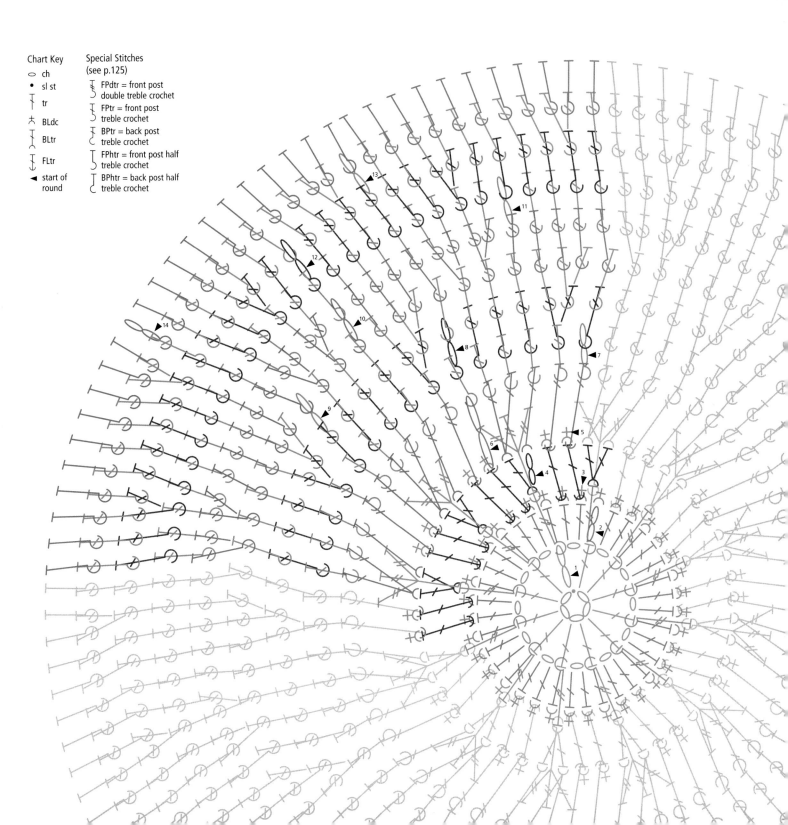

Chart Key

- ⌒ ch
- • sl st
- ⊤ tr
- 木 BLdc
- ⊤ BLtr
- ⊥ FLtr
- ◄ start of round

Special Stitches
(see p.125)

- FPdtr = front post double treble crochet
- FPtr = front post treble crochet
- BPtr = back post treble crochet
- FPhtr = front post half treble crochet
- BPhtr = back post half treble crochet

INSTRUCTIONS

SCALLOPS OF THE SEA

This is one of my favourite patterns. The widening rounds of shells create an enticing texture. Oh, and that modest border is ever so cute and clever.

Hook size: 3.5mm

Diameter: 18.5cm (7¼in)

To start (colour A): Make a magic ring or ch 10 and sl st in first ch to form a ring.

Round 1: 24 tr in ring.

Round 2 (colour B): *Tr in tr, ch 1; rep from * 23 more times. Join.

Round 3 (colour C): *Dc in tr, 3 tr in next tr (shell made); rep from * 11 more times. Join.

Round 4 (colour B): *Dc in 2nd tr of shell, skip next st, 5 tr in dc (shell made), skip next st; rep from * 11 more times. Join.

Round 5 (colour A): *Dc in 3rd tr of shell, skip next 2 sts, 5 tr in dc (shell made), skip next 2 sts; rep from * 11 more times. Join.

Round 6 (colour C): *Dc in 3rd tr of shell, skip next 2 sts, 7 tr in dc (shell made), skip next 2 sts; rep from * 11 more times. Join.

Round 7 (colour B): *Dc in 4th tr of shell, skip next 3 sts, 7 tr in dc (shell made), skip next 3 sts; rep from * 11 more times. Join.

Round 8 (colour A): *Dc in 4th tr of shell, skip next 3 sts, 7 dtr in dc (shell made), skip next 3 sts; rep from * 11 more times. Join.

Round 9 (colour C): *Dc in 4th dtr of shell, skip next 3 sts, 9 dtr in dc (shell made), skip next 3 sts; rep from * 11 more times. Join.

Round 10 (colour B): *Dc in 5th dtr of shell, ch 2, skip next 4 dtr, [(dtr, ch 1) six times, dtr, ch 2] in next dc, skip next 4 sts; rep from * 11 more times. Join.

Round 11 (colour C): *BPhtr in dc, ch 2, [BPhtr in next dtr, ch 1] six times, BPhtr in next dtr, ch 2; rep from * 11 more times. Join.

Fasten off. Weave in ends.

Chart Key
- ◯ ch
- • sl st
- ┬ tr
- + dc
- ┼ dtr
- ◀ start of round

Special Stitch (see p.125)
- ⊤ BPhtr = back post half
- ⊂ treble crochet

MAKE IT POP!

I just love this combination of popcorn stitches and openwork rounds. It gives this pretty mandala its most charming character.

Hook size: 3mm
Diameter: 19cm (7½in)

To start (colour A): Make a magic ring or ch 5 and sl st in first ch to form a ring.

Round 1: *Tr in ring, ch 1; rep from * 11 more times. Join.

Round 2 (colour B): *Tr2tog in ch-1 sp, ch 2; rep from * 11 more times. Join.

Round 3 (colour C): *Pc in ch-2 sp, ch 4; rep from * 11 more times. Join.

Round 4 (colour B): *5 tr in ch-4 sp, tr in pc; rep from * 11 more times. Join.

Round 5: *Tr in tr placed on top of pc, ch 7, skip next 5 sts; rep from * 11 more times. Join.

Round 6: *Dc in tr, 7 dc in ch-7 sp; rep from * 11 more times. Join.

Round 7 (colour A): BLtr in each st. Join.

Round 8 (colour B): *Dc in 7 sts, 2 dc in next st; rep from * 11 more times. Join.

Round 9: *Tr2tog in dc, ch 2, skip next st; rep from * 53 more times. Join.

Round 10 (colour C): *Pc in ch-2 sp, ch 2; rep from * 53 more times. Join.

Round 11 (colour B): *Tr in pc, 2 tr in ch-2 sp; rep from * 53 more times. Join.

Fasten off. Weave in ends.

Chart Key

○ ch
• sl st
† tr
tr2tog
+ dc
BLtr
◄ start of round

Special Stitch (see p.125)

pc = 5 tr popcorn

INSTRUCTIONS

DAINTY DAISY

Daisies rank high on the list of best-loved flowers, just as this cutie is highranking on my favourite mandala list. It's an easy pattern with a riveting result.

Hook size: 3mm
Diameter: 20.5cm (8in)

Chart Key
⌒ ch
• sl st
+ dc
⋔ tr4tog
⊤ tr
◄ start of round

To start (colour A): Make a magic ring or ch 5 and sl st in first ch to form a ring.

Round 1: 12 dc in ring. Join.

Round 2 (colour B): *Ch 13, sl st in next st; rep from * 11 more times. Join.

Round 3 (colour C): *Dc in ch-13 sp, ch 5; rep from * 11 more times. Join.

Round 4: *[Tr4tog, ch 3, tr4tog] in ch-5 sp, ch 3; rep from * 11 more times. Join.

Round 5 (colour D): *3 tr in ch-3 sp, tr in tr4tog cluster; rep from * 23 more times. Join.

Round 6 (colour C): *Dc in tr placed on top of tr4tog cluster, ch 4, skip next 3 tr; rep from * 23 more times. Join.

Round 7 (colour D): *4 tr in ch-4 sp, ch 1; rep from * 23 more times. Join.

Round 8 (colour E): *Tr4tog, ch 5; rep from * 23 more times. Join.

Round 9 (colour D): *[Tr4tog, ch 3, tr4tog] in ch-5 sp, ch 3, skip tr4tog; rep from * 23 more times. Join.

Round 10: *Dc in ch-3 sp between tr4tog clusters, in line with tr4tog from Round 8, 7 tr in next ch-3 sp; rep from * 23 more times. Join.

Fasten off. Weave in ends.

TULIPS FROM AMSTERDAM

A range of flower mandalas would not be complete without tulips, of course. I love everything about this mandala. The double-headed tulips in the centre are a pretty and unique detail.

Hook size: 3mm
Diameter: 24cm (9½in)

To start (colour A): Make a magic ring or ch 6 and sl st in first ch to form a ring.

Round 1: 12 dc in ring. Join.

Round 2 (colour B): *2 htr in each st. Join.

Round 3 (colour C): *[Tr, ch 4, tr] in htr, skip next 2 htr; rep from * seven more times. Join.

Round 4 (colour D): *[Tr3tog, ch 3, tr3tog] in ch-4 sp, ch 3; rep from * seven more times. Join.

Round 5 (colour B): *3 htr in ch-3 sp, htr in tr3tog cluster; rep from * 15 more times. Join.

Round 6: *Htr in 7 sts, 2 htr in next st; rep from * seven more times. Join.

Round 7 (colour C): *[Tr, ch 3, tr] in htr, skip next 2 htr; rep from * 23 more times. Join.

Round 8 (colour E): *Tr4tog in ch-3 sp, ch 4; rep from * 23 more times. Join.

Round 9 (colour B): *Htr in tr4tog cluster, 4 htr in ch-4 sp; rep from * 23 more times. Join.

Round 10: *Htr in each st. Join.

Round 11 (colour C): *[Tr, ch 2, tr] in htr, skip next 2 htr; rep from * 39 more times. Join.

Round 12 (colour F): *Tr4tog in ch-2 sp, ch 4; rep from * 39 more times. Join.

Round 13 (colour B): *Htr in tr4tog cluster; 3 htr in ch-4 sp; rep from * 39 more times. Join.

Round 14: *Htr in 7 sts, 2 htr in next st; rep from * 19 more times. Join.

Round 15: *Dc in next st, skip next 2 htr, [(tr, picot-3, ch 1) three times, tr] in next st, skip next 2 htr; rep from * 29 more times. Join.

Fasten off. Weave in ends.

Chart Key	Special Stitch (see p.125)
⌒ ch	✿ picot-3
• sl st	
+ dc	
⊤ htr	
𝙼 tr3tog	
⊺ tr	
𝙼 tr4tog	
◀ start of round	

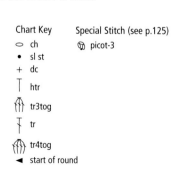

AFRICAN FLOWER LOVE

The African Flower is a much-loved classic in the crochet world so I definitely wanted to design a mandala based on this marvellous motif – and I just love how it turned out!

Hook size: 3mm
Diameter: 18.5cm (7¼in)

To start (colour A): Make a magic ring or ch 5 and sl st in first ch to form a ring.

Round 1: *2 tr in ring, ch 1; rep from * five more times. Join.

Round 2 (colour B): [2 tr, ch 1, 2 tr] in each ch-1 sp. Join.

Round 3 (colour A): 7 tr in each ch-1 sp. Join.

Round 4 (colour C): *Dc in 7 tr, dc in point where 2 tr and 2 tr 'meet' in Round 2 (long dc); rep from * five more times. Join.

Round 5: *Dc in long dc, ch 4, skip next 3 dc, dc in next dc, ch 4, skip next 3 dc; rep from * five more times. Join.

Round 6 (colour B): [2 tr, ch 2, 2 tr] in each ch-4 sp. Join.

Round 7 (colour D): 7 tr in each ch-2 sp. Join.

Round 8 (colour E): *Dc in 7 tr, long dc in point where 2 tr and 2 tr 'meet' in Round 6; rep from * 11 more times. Join.

Round 9: *Dc in long dc, ch 4, skip next 3 dc, dc in next dc, ch 4, skip next 3 dc; rep from * 11 more times. Join.

Round 10: *Dc in ch-4 sp, ch 5; rep from * 23 more times. Join.

Round 11 (colour A): 5 tr in each ch-5 sp. Join.

Round 12 (colour E): *Dc in 5 tr, long dc in dc in Round 10; rep from * 23 more times. Join.

Round 13 (colour A): BLtr in each st. Join.

Round 14 (colour E): Crab st in each st. Join.

Fasten off. Weave in ends.

Chart Key
- ◠ ch
- • sl st
- ⊤ tr
- + dc
- ⊥ BLtr
- ◄ start of round

Special Stitch (see p.125)
- ⌇ crab st

ORIENTAL LILY

I dote on this delicate mandala. The centre of this mandala (up to Round 5) would also work very well on its own if you are looking for a small circle motif.

Hook size: 3mm
Diameter: 19.5cm
(7¾in)

To start (colour A): Make a magic ring or ch 6 and sl st in first ch to form a ring.

Round 1: *Dtr3tog in ring, ch 3; rep from * seven more times. Join.

Round 2 (colour B): *[Dtr3tog, ch 3, dtr3tog] in ch-3 sp, ch 3; rep from * seven more times. Join.

Round 3: *3 dc in ch-3 sp, dc in dtr3tog cluster; rep from * 15 more times. Join.

Round 4 (colour C): BLdc in each st. Join.

Round 5 (colour B): BLdc in each st. Join.

Round 6: *Dc in dc, ch 5, skip next 3 dc; rep from * 15 more times. Join.

Round 7 (colour D): *Dc in ch-5 sp, ch 2, 9 tr in next ch-5 sp (shell made), ch 2; rep from * seven more times. Join.

Round 8: *Dc in first tr of shell, ch 5, skip next 3 tr, dc in next tr, ch 5, skip next 3 tr, dc in next tr, ch 5, skip next dc; rep from * seven more times. Join.

Round 9: *Dc in ch-5 sp, ch 5, dc in next ch-5 sp, ch 2, 9 tr in next ch-5 sp (shell made), ch 2; rep from * seven more times. Join.

Round 10: *2 tr in first tr of shell, [tr in next 3 sts, 2 tr in next st] twice, ch 1, [tr, ch 3, tr] in next ch-5 sp, ch 1; rep from * seven more times. Join.

Round 11: *2 tr in first tr of shell, tr in next 10 sts, 2 tr in next st, ch 1, [tr, ch 3, tr] in ch-3 sp, ch 1; rep from * seven more times. Join.

Round 12: *Dc in each tr of shell (14 dc), ch 3, [tr, ch 3, tr] in ch-3 sp, ch 3; rep from * seven more times. Join.

Fasten off. Weave in ends.

Chart Key

- ◦ ch
- • sl st
- dtr3tog
- ⋏ BLdc
- + dc
- † tr
- ◄ start of round

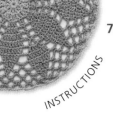

LEAVES AND LACE

This is an amazingly versatile mandala. If you love it as much as I do, have a look at the projects section for a beautiful blanket pattern made with this motif on pages 120–123.

Hook size: 3mm
Diameter: 21.5cm
(8½in)

To start (colour A): Make a magic ring or ch 4 and sl st in first ch to form a ring.

Round 1: *Tr in ring, ch 1; rep from * 11 more times. Join.

Round 2: *2 tr in tr, ch 1; rep from * 11 more times. Join.

Round 3 (colour B): *Tr2tog, ch 3, tr in next tr, 2 tr in next tr, ch 3; rep from * five more times. Join.

Round 4: *Tr in tr2tog cluster, ch 3, 2 tr in next tr, tr in next st, 2 tr in next st, ch 3; rep from * five more times. Join.

Round 5: *Tr in tr between two ch-3 sps, ch 3, 2 tr in next tr, [tr in next st, 2 tr in next st] twice, ch 3; rep from * five more times. Join.

Round 6: *[Tr, ch 3, tr] in tr between two ch-3 sps, ch 3, tr in next 8 tr, ch 3; rep from * five more times. Join.

Round 7: *Tr in first tr of Round 6, 3 tr in ch-3 sp, tr in next tr, ch 3, tr2tog, tr in next 4 sts, tr2tog, ch 3; rep from * five more times. Join.

Round 8: *2 tr in first tr of Round 7, [tr in next st, 2 tr in next st] twice, ch 5, tr2tog, tr in next 2 sts, tr2tog, ch 5; rep from * five more times. Join.

Round 9: *Tr2tog in first and 2nd sts of Round 8, [tr in next st, tr2tog] twice, ch 5, dc in ch-5 sp, ch 5, [tr2tog] twice, ch 5, dc in ch-5 sp, ch 5; rep from * five more times. Join.

Round 10: *Tr2tog in first and 2nd sts of Round 9, tr in next st, tr2tog, ch 5, dc in ch-5 sp, ch 5, skip next dc, dc in ch-5 sp, ch 5, tr2tog, ch 5, dc in ch-5 sp, ch 5, skip next dc, dc in ch-5 sp, ch 5; rep from * five more times. Join.

Round 11: *Tr3tog in first 3 sts of Round 10, ch 5, dc in ch-5 sp, [ch 5, skip next st, dc in ch-5 sp] five times, ch 5; rep from * five more times. Join.

Round 12: *Dc in ch-5 sp, ch 5; rep from * 41 more times. Join.

Round 13 (colour C): *Dc in ch-5 sp, ch 5; rep from * 41 more times. Join.

Fasten off. Weave in ends.

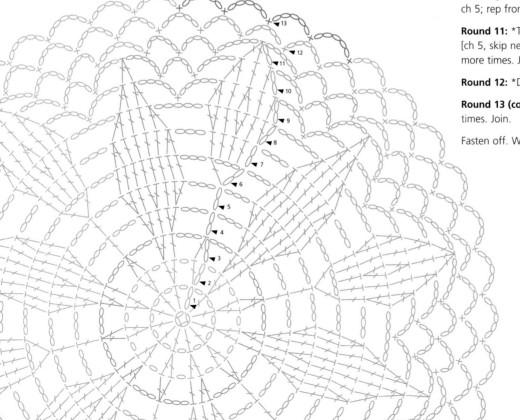

Chart Key
⌒ ch
• sl st
† tr
⋏ tr2tog
+ dc
⋔ tr3tog
◄ start of round

STRAWBERRY BLOSSOM

This mandala has a certain *je ne sais quoi* about it. Could it possibly have something to do with that adorable border?

Hook size: 3mm
Diameter: 21cm (8¼in)

To start (colour A): Make a magic ring or ch 5 and sl st in first ch to form a ring.

Round 1: 12 dc in ring. Join.

Round 2: *Tr in dc, ch 3, skip next dc; rep from * five more times. Join.

Round 3: *[Dc, 2 tr, dtr, 2 tr, dc] in ch-3 sp; rep from * five more times. Join.

Round 4 (colour B): BLtr in 2nd dc, BLhtr in next st, BLdc in next 3 sts, BLhtr in next st, BLtr in next st; rep from * five more times. Join.

Round 5: *Tr in 2 sts, 2 tr in next st; rep from * 13 more times. Join.

Round 6 (colour C): *[Tr2tog, ch 5, tr2tog] in tr, ch 1, skip next 3 tr; rep from * 13 more times. Join.

Round 7 (colour B): *Dc in ch-1 sp, ch 1, 5 tr in ch-5 sp, ch 1; rep from * 13 more times. Join.

Round 8 (colour C): *Dc in 3rd tr, [tr2tog, ch 6, tr2tog] in next dc; rep from * 13 more times. Join.

Round 9 (colour B): *Dc in dc, 9 tr in ch-6 sp; rep from * 13 more times. Join.

Round 10 (colour C): *[Tr2tog, ch 6, tr2tog] in 5th tr, ch 6; rep from * 13 more times. Join.

Round 11 (colour B): *13 tr in ch-6 sp between two paired tr2tog clusters, dc in next ch-6 sp; rep from * 13 more times. Join.

Round 12: *BLdc in 13 tr, dc in dc, ch 7, sl st in same dc; rep from * 13 more times. Join.

Fasten off.

Round 13 (colour A): This is not a continuous round, but is worked separately in every ch-7 sp of Round 12. *[Dc, ch 3, dc, ch 3, dc] in ch-7 sp, fasten off; rep from * 13 more times.

Weave in ends.

Chart Key
⌒ ch
• sl st
+ dc
† tr
‡ dtr
BLtr
BLhtr
tr2tog
BLdc
◄ start of round

SAY IT WITH FLOWERS

There's definitely a lot of expression and personality in this flowery mandala. The repetitive rounds combining both dense and openwork petals give this mandala an unusual, layered effect.

Hook size: 3mm
Diameter: 22.5cm
(8¾in)

To start (colour A): Make a magic ring or ch 9 and sl st in first ch to form a ring.

Round 1: 24 tr in ring. Join.

Round 2 (colour B): *Tr2tog in tr, ch 3, skip next tr; rep from * 11 more times. Join.

Round 3 (colour C): *Tr in tr2tog cluster, 3 tr in ch-3 sp; rep from * 11 more times. Join.

Round 4: *Dc in tr placed on top of tr2tog cluster, skip next tr, 5 tr in next tr (shell made), skip next tr; rep from * 11 more times. Join.

Round 5 (colour A): *BLdc in 3rd tr of shell, BLhtr in next st, BLtr in next 3 sts, BLhtr in next st; rep from * 11 more times. Join.

Round 6: *Dc in middle tr of group of 3 tr, skip next 2 sts, 9 tr in dc (shell made), skip next 2 sts; rep from * 11 more times. Join.

Round 7 (colour B): *Dc in 5th tr of shell, ch 3, skip next 4 tr, [tr, ch 9, tr] in dc, ch 3, skip next 4 tr; rep from * 11 more times. Join.

Round 8 (colour C): *Dc in dc, 15 tr in ch-9 sp; rep from * 11 more times. Join.

Round 9 (colour B): *Dc in tr, ch 5, skip next 7 tr, dtr in dc, ch 5, skip next 7 tr; rep from * 11 more times. Join. Note that in this round, your mandala might 'cup' a little bit – this will be corrected in the next round.

Round 10: *Tr in dtr, 5 tr in ch-5 sp, tr in dc, 5 tr in ch-5 sp; rep from * 11 more times. Join.

Round 11: *Tr in 7 sts, 2 tr in next st; rep from * 17 more times.

Round 12: *Tr in 8 sts, 2 tr in next st; rep from * 17 more times. Join.

Round 13 (colour C): *Dc in each st. Join.

Round 14 (colour B): Use a larger hook for this round. For instance, if you have worked this mandala using a 3mm hook, you should switch to at least a 3.5mm hook for this round. *BLsl st in each st. Join.

Fasten off. Weave in ends.

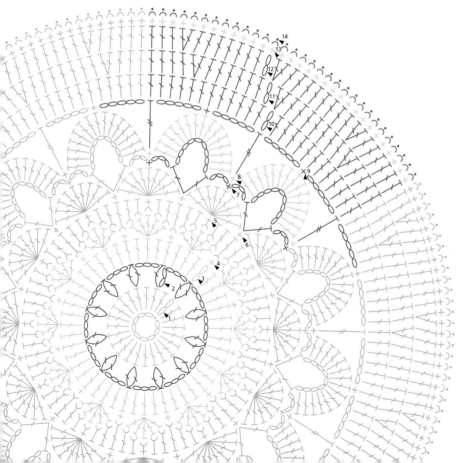

Chart Key

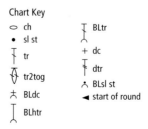

⌒	ch	⊥	BLtr
•	sl st	+	dc
⊤	tr		dtr
	tr2tog	⋏	BLsl st
⋏	BLdc	◄	start of round
	BLhtr		

FIELD OF WILD FLOWERS

This mandala is the next best thing to walking barefoot through a field of flowers on a lazy afternoon. Making the little flowers is quite addictive, so I wouldn't be surprised if you end up with lots and lots of them.

Hook size: 3.5mm
Diameter: 20.5cm (8in)

Chart Key
⌒ ch
• sl st
+ dc
⊤ htr
◄ start of round

Special Stitch
(see p.125)
⊕ pc = 5 tr popcorn

Note:
This mandala has nine flowers. The central flower is created in Rounds 1–2. Use the Rounds 1–2 instructions and chart to make eight additional flowers in the colours of your choice.

Flower

To start (colour A): Make a magic ring or ch 4 and sl st in first ch to form a ring.

Round 1: 6 dc in ring. Join.

Round 2 (colour B): *[Sl st, ch 3, pc, ch 3, sl st] in each st. Join.

Mandala

Round 3 (colour C): *Dc at back of pc (do not work dc in top of pc, but just below), ch 3; rep from * five more times. Join.

Round 4: *5 dc in ch-3 sp, dc in dc; rep from * five more times. Join.

Round 5: *Dc in 6 sts, 2 dc in next st; rep from * four more times. Join.

Round 6: *Dc in 7 sts, 2 dc in next st; rep from * four more times. Join.

Round 7: Attach 8 flowers to Round 6, either by slip stitching while making the flowers, or sewing the flowers once they are complete. Refer to the chart for where to work the stitches.

Round 8 (colour C): Start this round in the first of the two top petals on the outer side of your work. *Dc at back of pc (do not work dc in top of pc, but just below), ch 3, dc in next pc, ch 6; rep from * seven more times. Join.

Round 9: *5 htr in ch-3 sp, htr in dc, 8 htr in ch-6 sp, htr in dc; rep from * seven more times. Join.

Round 10: Htr in each st. Join.

Round 11 (colour A): *Dc in htr, ch 2, skip next 2 htr; rep from * 39 more times. Join.

Round 12 (colour C): *3 htr in ch-2 sp; rep from * 39 more times. Join.

Round 13 (colour A): *Dc in sp between two 3-htr clusters, ch 3; rep from * 39 more times. Join.

Round 14 (colour C): *4 htr in ch-3 sp; rep from * 39 more times. Join.

Round 15 (colour A): *Dc in sp between two 4-htr clusters, ch 4; rep from * 39 more times. Join.

Fasten off. Weave in ends.

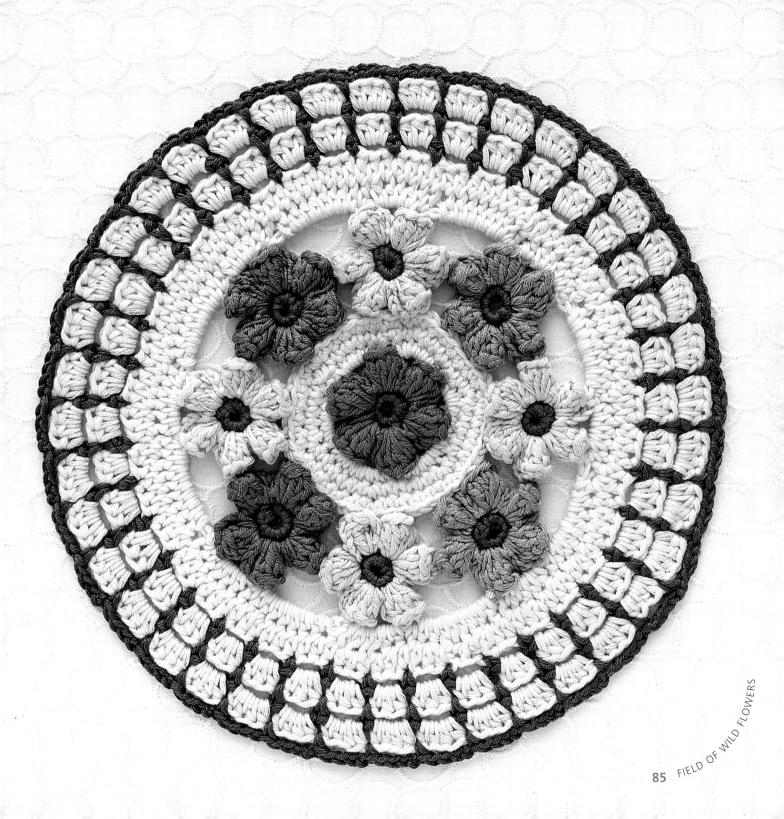

LOVE ME LOOPS

The rich and soft texture of this mandala is incredible. You'll want to cuddle your work – that's a promise. The first loop stitches can be a bit fiddly, but after that it's easy peasy because, although it might look complex, this technique is based on the modest double crochet stitch.

Hook size: 3.5mm
Diameter: 14cm (5½in)

Notes:

• This mandala is worked from the back, and the loops then appear on the front of the work. The pattern calls for double loop stitches, so each stitch creates two loops, giving the mandala a very soft and tactile texture.

• It's advisable to use stitch markers to mark the first stitch of each round. With all the loops, it can be difficult to recognise.

To start (colour A): Make a magic ring or ch 4 and sl st in first ch to form a ring.

Round 1: 6 dc in ring. Join.

Round 2: *2 db lp in each st. Join.

Round 3: *Db lp in first st, 2 db lp in next st; rep from * five more times. Join.

Round 4 (colour B): *Db lp in 2 sts, 2 db lp in next st; rep from * five more times. Join.

Round 5: *Db lp in 3 sts, 2 db lp in next st; rep from * five more times. Join.

Round 6 (colour C): *Db lp in 4 sts, 2 db lp in next st; rep from * five more times. Join.

Round 7: *Db lp in 5 sts, 2 db lp in next st; rep from * five more times. Join.

Round 8: *Db lp in 6 sts, 2 db lp in next st; rep from * five more times. Join.

Round 9 (colour D): *Db lp in 7 sts, 2 db lp in next st; rep from * five more times. Join.

Round 10 (colour E): *Db lp in 8 sts, 2 db lp in next st; rep from * five more times. Join.

Round 11: *Db lp in 9 sts, 2 db lp in next st; rep from * five more times. Join.

Round 12 (colour F): *Db lp in 10 sts, 2 db lp in next st; rep from * five more times. Join.

Fasten off. Weave in ends.

Chart Key

⌒ ch
• sl st
+ dc
◄ start of round

Special Stitches (see p.125)

ᕈ db lp = double loop stitch
ᕧ 2 db lp = two double loop stitches

LAYERS AND LOOPS

I love how the loops in this pattern are picked up by stitches in later rounds, giving this mandala a delightful dynamic. It's not a difficult pattern, but it does need some concentration to get it right.

Hook size: 3mm

Diameter: 18.5cm (7¼in)

To start (colour A): Make a magic ring or ch 4 and sl st in first ch to form a ring.

Round 1: 8 dc in ring. Join.

Round 2: 2 dc in each st. Join. (16 dc.)

Round 3: *Dc in st, 2 dc in next st; rep from * seven more times. Join. (24 dc.)

Round 4 (colour B): *Dc in st, ch 8, skip next 2 sts; rep from * seven more times. Join.

Round 5 (colour A): *5 tr in ch-8 sp, ch 2; rep from * seven more times. Join.

Round 6: *5 tr in ch-2 sp, ch 5; rep from * seven more times. Join.

Round 7: *Tr in 2nd tr, tr in next 2 sts, ch 3, 3 tr in ch-5 sp, ch 3; rep from * seven more times. Join.

Round 8 (colour B): Worked in sts of Rounds 5 and 6. *On Round 5: tr in 2nd tr, tr in next 2 sts. Sl st in ch-5 sp of Round 6, ch 8, sl st in next ch-5 sp of Round 6; rep from * seven more times. Join.

Round 9 (colour A): Worked in sts of Round 7. *3 tr in ch-3 sp, tr in next st, pick up ch-8 loop of Round 8 to secure and make tr in next st, tr in next st; rep from * seven more times. Join.

Round 10 (colour C): *Tr in 3 sts, 2 tr in next st; rep from * 23 more times. Join.

Round 11: *Tr4tog in st, ch 3, skip next 2 sts; rep from * 39 more times. Join.

Round 12 (colour B): *Dc in ch-3 sp, ch 4; rep from * 39 more times. Join.

Round 13 (colour D): *Dc in ch-4 sp, ch 3, dc in same ch-4 sp, ch 2; rep from * 39 more times. Join.

Fasten off. Weave in ends.

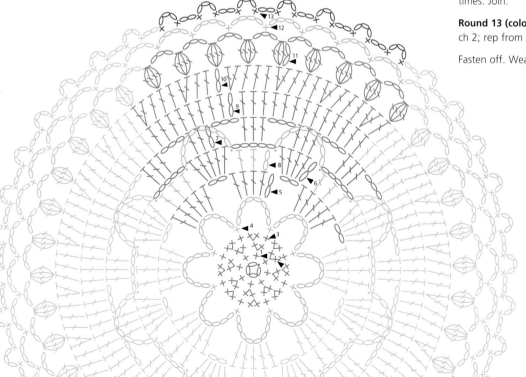

Chart Key

⌒ ch

• sl st

+ dc

╁ tr

⬦ tr4tog

◄ start of round

INSTRUCTIONS

CONFETTI TIME!

You can make this beauty as big as you like simply by adding more mini mandalas and following the same pattern. Why not create it in T-shirt yarn for a snuggly and eye-catching floor mat?

Hook size: 3.5mm
Diameter: 14.5cm
(5¾in)

Notes:
• To make this mandala, you need to make 37 small circles. To match the design shown here,

Make: 1 × colour A
6 × colour B
12 × colour C
18 × colour D

You can either join them as you go or stitch them together at the end.

• You can make this mandala as large as you want by adding more rounds. Increase the number of circles by six for each additional round.

To start: Make a magic ring or ch 4 and sl st in first ch to form a ring.

Round 1: 12 tr in ring.

Fasten off. Weave in ends.

Assembling:

To join as you go: Use the chart as reference for where to join the circles. When making Circle 2, you need to join it to Circle 1 as you start making the tr. Work: [yo, insert hook in ring of Circle 2 and pull yarn through, yo, pull through 2 loops on hook], then (before completing the tr) put the hook through the back loop of the corresponding stitch of Circle 1 and complete the treble crochet. The circles are now joined. Continue like this with all the circles.

To sew the mandala together: Make all 37 circles, then arrange them in the order you want to join them. Using a blunt needle, stitch them together through the back loops only.

Chart Key
○ ch
• sl st
† tr
– Joining points

ENCHANTED APRIL

If you are an admirer of the popcorn stitch – I know I am – you'll have a ball with this pattern. It's fascinating that with just a hook and some yarn, you can easily create this delightful texture.

Hook size: 3.5mm
Diameter: 22.5cm
(8¾in)

Note:
Since the sections of this pattern have gaps between them, you can place the first st of each round on top of the first st of the previous round without leaving a visible line of starting stitches.

To start (colour A): Make a magic ring or ch 4 and sl st in first ch to form a ring.

Round 1: *Tr in ring, ch 2; rep from * seven more times. Join.

Round 2 (colour B): *Tr3tog in ch-2 sp, ch 4; rep from * seven more times. Join.

Round 3 (colour C): *[Tr, ch 2, pc, ch 2, tr, ch 2] in ch-4 sp; rep from * seven more times. Join.

Round 4: *Tr in tr, [ch 2, pc in next ch-2 sp] twice, ch 2, tr in next st, ch 2; rep from * seven more times. Join.

Round 5: *Tr in tr, [ch 2, pc in next ch-2 sp] three times, ch 2, tr in next st, ch 2; rep from * seven more times. Join.

Round 6: *Tr in tr, [ch 2, pc in next ch-2 sp] four times, ch 2, tr in next st, ch 2; rep from * seven more times. Join.

Round 7: *Tr in tr, [ch 2, pc in next ch-2 sp] five times, ch 2, tr in next st, ch 2; rep from * seven more times. Join.

Round 8: *Tr in tr, [ch 2, pc in next ch-2 sp] six times, ch 2, tr in next st, ch 2; rep from * seven more times. Join.

Round 9: *Tr in tr, [ch 2, pc in next ch-2 sp] seven times, ch 2, tr in next st, ch 2; rep from * seven more times. Join.

Round 10 (colour B): *Tr in tr, [ch 2, pc in next ch-2 sp] eight times, ch 2, tr in next st, ch 2; rep from * seven more times. Join.

Fasten off. Weave in ends.

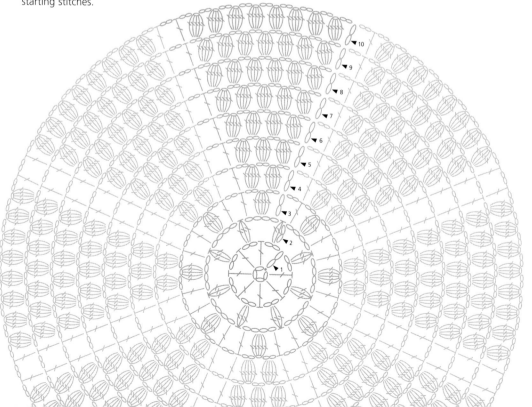

Chart Key
⌒ ch
• sl st
╀ tr
⬙ tr3tog
◄ start of round

Special Stitch (see p.125)
⬙ pc = 5 tr popcorn

INSTRUCTIONS

DAZZLING DAYS

If you've never had a go at tapestry (or jacquard) crochet, this is a great pattern for your first time. With this basic but versatile technique you'll make this striking mandala in no time – and you'll love the dense texture of this one!

Hook size: 3mm
Diameter: 23cm (9in)

Special Abbreviation
chg to A (or B) = change to colour A (or B) for the final 'yo, pull through' of the last stitch worked.

Notes:
- For this technique you carry two colours/strands of yarn simultaneously. The colour that is not in use is run along the back of the stitches and picked up again when needed.

- When the pattern indicates that a colour change is coming up, you begin to work the last tr in the first colour as usual, but do the last yarn over with the second colour (and drop the first). Then work the indicated tr in the second colour. When you need to return to the first colour, begin making the last tr in the second colour, but finish it with the first. So basically: you start working with the new colour just before the chart and pattern indicate this by finishing the last tr in the new colour.

To start (colour A): Make a magic ring or ch 6 and sl st in first ch to form a ring.

Round 1 (colours A and B): *Tr (A) in ring, chg to B for last yo to finish first tr, tr (B) in ring, chg to A for last yo to finish tr; rep from * seven more times. Join. You now have a basic circle of 16 dc with colours A and B alternating.

Round 2: *2 tr (A) in any colour A tr, chg to B, 2 tr in next st, chg to A; rep from * seven more times. Join.

Round 3: *Tr (A) in first st of any group of colour A sts, 2 tr in next st, chg to B, tr in next st, 2 tr in next st, chg to A; rep from * seven more times. Join.

Round 4: *Tr (A) in first 2 sts of any group of colour A sts, 2 tr in next st, chg to B, tr in next 2 sts, 2 tr in next st, chg to A; rep from * seven more times. Join.

Round 5: *Tr (A) in first 3 sts of any group of colour A sts, 2 tr in next st, chg to B, tr in next 3 sts, 2 tr in next st, chg to A; rep from * seven more times. Join.

Round 6: *Tr (A) in 2nd st of any group of colour A sts, tr in next 2 sts, chg to B, tr in next st, 2 tr in next st, tr in next 4 sts, 2 tr in next st, chg to A; rep from * seven more times. Join.

Round 7: *Tr (A) in 2nd st of any group of colour A sts, chg to B, tr in next st, 2 tr in next st, tr in next 5 sts, 2 tr in next st, tr in next 3 sts, chg to A; rep from * seven more times. Join.

Round 8: *2 tr (B) in 2nd st of any group of colour B sts, tr in next 6 sts, 2 tr in next st, tr in next 3 sts, chg to A, tr in next 3 sts, chg to B; rep from * seven more times. Join.

Round 9: *Tr (B) in 2nd st of any group of colour B sts, tr in next st, 2 tr in next st, tr in next 7 sts, 2 tr in next st, chg to A, tr in next 5 sts, chg to B; rep from * seven more times. Join.

Round 10: *Tr (B) in 2nd st of any group of colour B sts, 2 tr in next st, tr in next 8 sts, 2 tr in next st, chg to A, tr in next 7 sts, chg to B; rep from * seven more times. Join.

Round 11: *2 tr (B) in 2nd st of any group of colour B sts, tr in next 9 sts, 2 tr in next st, chg to A, tr in next 9 sts, chg to B; rep from * seven more times. Join.

Round 12: *Tr (B) in 2nd st of any group of colour B sts, tr in next 3 sts, 2 tr in next st, tr in next 6 sts, chg to A, tr in next 4 sts, 2 tr in next st, tr in next 6 sts, chg to B; rep from * seven more times. Join.

Fasten off. Weave in ends.

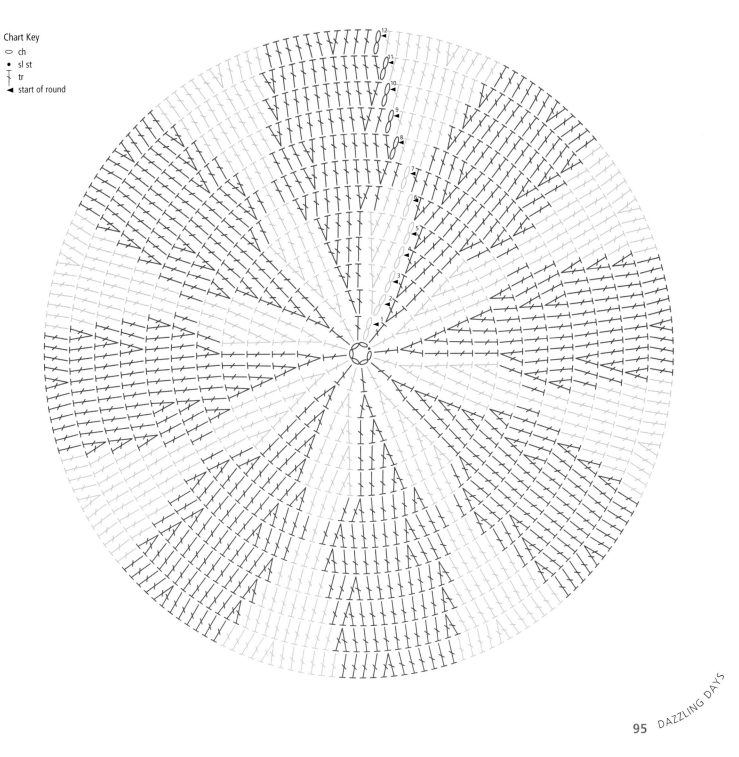

INSTRUCTIONS

VINTAGE VIBES

Can I say I'm really proud of this mandala? Small in size, huge in prettiness – that's this mandala in a few words. Granted it's not the easiest pattern in this book, but it is oh so worth the effort!

Hook size: 3mm
Diameter: 13.5cm
(5¼in)

Note:
Additional colours have been used in this chart for added clarity.

To start (colour A): Make a magic ring or ch 5 and sl st in first ch to form a ring.

Round 1: *Tr in ring, ch 1; rep from * 11 more times. Join.

Round 2 (colour B): *Tr3tog in ch-1 sp, ch 3; rep from * 11 more times. Join.

Round 3 (colour C): *5 tr in ch-3 sp; rep from * 11 more times. Join.

Round 4 (colour A): *BLdc in 4th tr of any 5-tr cluster, BLdc in next 3 sts, FPquadtr in tr of Round 1; rep from * 11 more times. Join.

Round 5 (colour C): *2 tr in FPquadtr, FLtr in next 4 tr of Round 3; rep from * 11 more times. Join.

Round 6 (colour A): *3 FPdtr in FPquadtr of Round 4; BLdc in next 4 tr; rep from * 11 more times. Join.

Round 7 (colour C): Please note: in this round you'll be using both FLtr and BLtr stitches. The back loop stitches are worked in the 2 tr behind the 3-FPdtr clusters; the front loop stitches are worked in the 4 tr in between the FPdtr clusters. This round is worked in the sts of Round 5. *BLtr in first tr of Round 5 behind 3-FPdtr cluster, BLtr in next tr of Round 5, FLtr in next 4 tr of Round 5; rep from * 11 more times. Join.

Round 8 (colour A): *Dc between 2nd and 3rd FLtr of Round 7, ch 3, dtr3tog in 3 FPdtr of Round 6, ch 3; rep from * 11 more times. Join.

Round 9 (colour B): *Dc in dtr3tog cluster, 3 dc in ch-3 sp, FPsextr in tr3tog cluster of Round 2, 3 dc in ch-3 sp; rep from * 11 more times. Join.

Round 10: *Dc in dc placed on top of dtr3tog cluster, ch 5, skip next 3 dc, tr3tog in FPsextr, ch 5, skip next 3 dc; rep from * 11 more times. Join.

Round 11 (colour A): *Dc in top of tr3tog cluster, picot-3, 5 dc in ch-5 sp, FPtr2tog in dtr3tog of Round 8, 5 dc in ch-5 sp; rep from * 11 more times. Join.

Fasten off. Weave in ends.

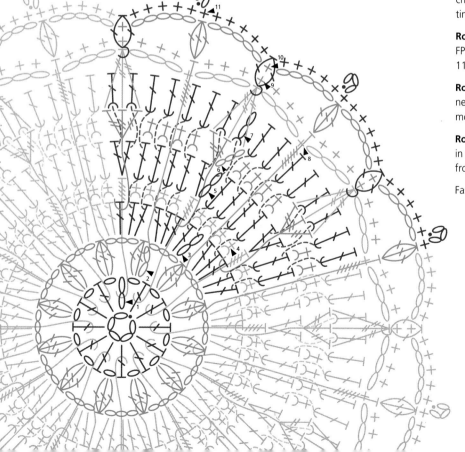

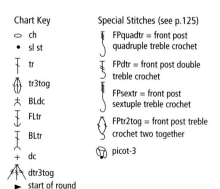

Chart Key		Special Stitches (see p.125)
⌒ ch		FPquadtr = front post quadruple treble crochet
• sl st		
ꓕ tr		FPdtr = front post double treble crochet
tr3tog		
BLdc		FPsextr = front post sextuple treble crochet
FLtr		
BLtr		FPtr2tog = front post treble crochet two together
+ dc		
dtr3tog		picot-3
▶ start of round		

DELIGHTFUL DOILY

This is another favourite! There's something undeniably charming in the combination of the puff stitches and the quirky border. Pay special attention to where you work the double crochets in the border.

Hook size: 3.5mm
Diameter: 19.5cm (7¾in)

Note:
The first puff st of a round can be made a standing puff st by working a yarn over, securing the loop with your finger on the hook and completing the puff st as usual.

To start (colour A): Make a magic ring or ch 4 and sl st in first ch to form a ring.

Round 1: 8 dc in ring. Join.

Round 2: *Puff in dc, ch 3; rep from * seven more times. Join.

Round 3 (colour B): *Dc in puff st, 3 dc in ch-3 sp; rep from * seven more times. Join.

Round 4: *Puff in dc above puff st, ch 2, skip next dc; rep from * 15 more times. Join.

Round 5 (colour A): *Dc in puff st, 2 dc in ch-2 sp; rep from * 15 more times. Join.

Chart Key
- ◠ ch
- • sl st
- + dc
- ◄ start of round

Special Stitch
(see p.125)
- ⬯ puff = puff stitch

Round 6: *Puff in dc above puff st, ch 2, skip next dc; rep from * 23 more times. Join.

Round 7 (colour B): *Dc in puff st, 2 dc in ch-2 sp; rep from * 23 more times. Join.

Round 8: *Puff in dc above puff st, ch 2, skip next dc; rep from * 35 more times. Join.

Round 9 (colour A): *Dc in puff st, 2 dc in ch-2 sp; rep from * 35 more times. Join.

Round 10: *Puff in dc above puff st, ch 2, skip next 2 dc; rep from * 35 more times. Join.

Round 11 (colour B): *Dc in puff st, 3 dc in ch-2 sp; rep from * 35 more times. Join.

Note: To create the vertical zigzag effect with the dc sts in Rounds 12–17, insert your hook in the dc of the previous round lower than you normally would. Work the dc between the V of that dc.

Round 12 (colour A): *Dc in dc above puff st, ch 3, skip next 3 dc; rep from * 35 more times. Join.

Round 13 (colour B): *Dc in dc, ch 3; rep from * 35 more times. Join.

Round 14 (colour A): *Dc in dc, ch 4; rep from * 35 more times. Join.

Round 15 (colour B): *Dc in dc, ch 4; rep from * 35 more times. Join.

Round 16 (colour A): *Dc in dc, ch 4; rep from * 35 more times. Join.

Round 17 (colour B): *Dc in dc, ch 5; rep from * 35 more times. Join.

Round 18 (colour A): *Dc in dc, ch 5; rep from * 35 more times. Join.

Fasten off. Weave in ends.

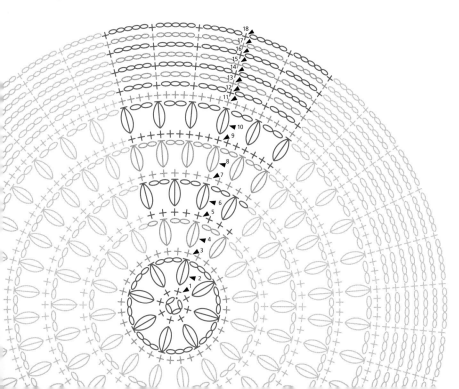

BORDERS

I've designed five borders for you that will turn the most basic mandala into a work of beauty. To let the borders speak for themselves, I've used a really simple mandala as the basis: Rounds 1–12 of the 'Handsome Hoops' mandala on page 42. If your mandala has a different number of stitches in the last round, you can easily adapt these border patterns to fit. For that you can use the tips on page 19 for keeping your circles flat.

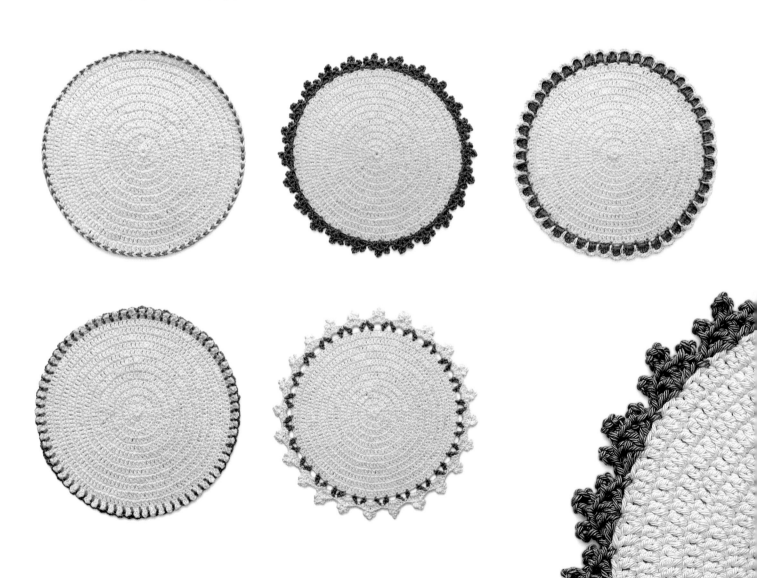

Grace Border

This simple yet effective border is worked with two colours simultanuously. Switch to a slightly larger hook for the border to prevent your mandala from cupping.

Make a sl st with colour A, then pull colour B through the st and make a sl st while securing colour A with your finger behind the work. Secure colour B and make a sl st with colour A.

Continue all around, alternating colours. Join with a blunt needle to make a seamless join and weave in ends.

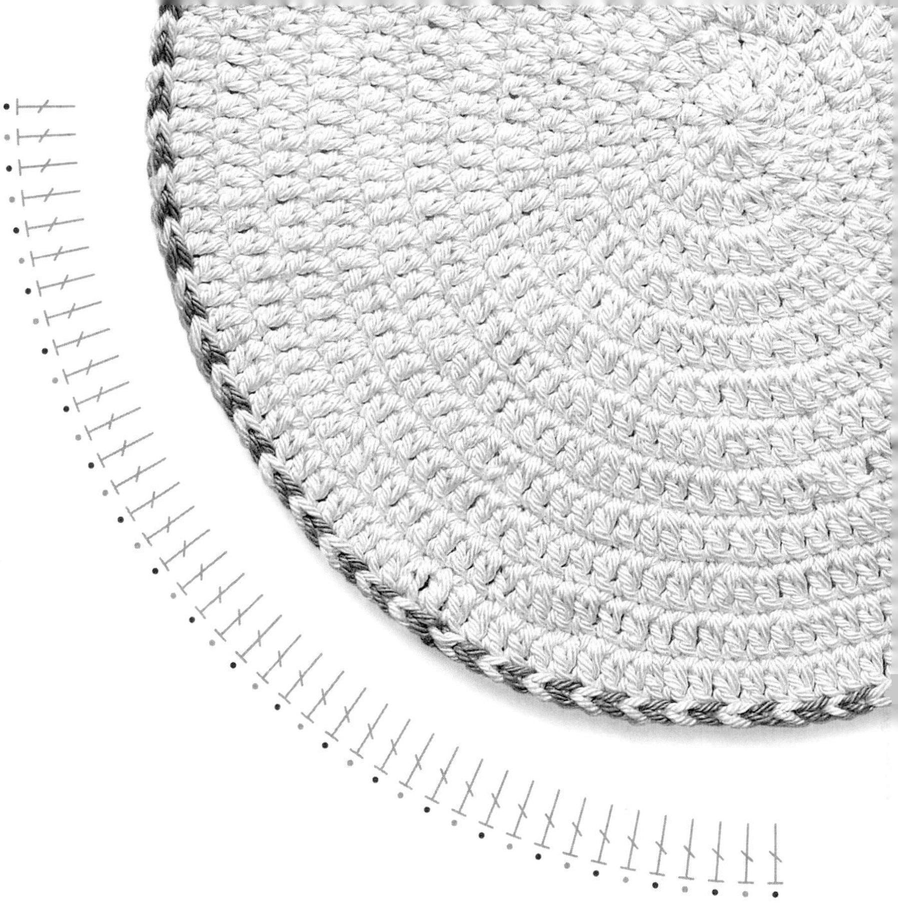

Chart Key
● sl st

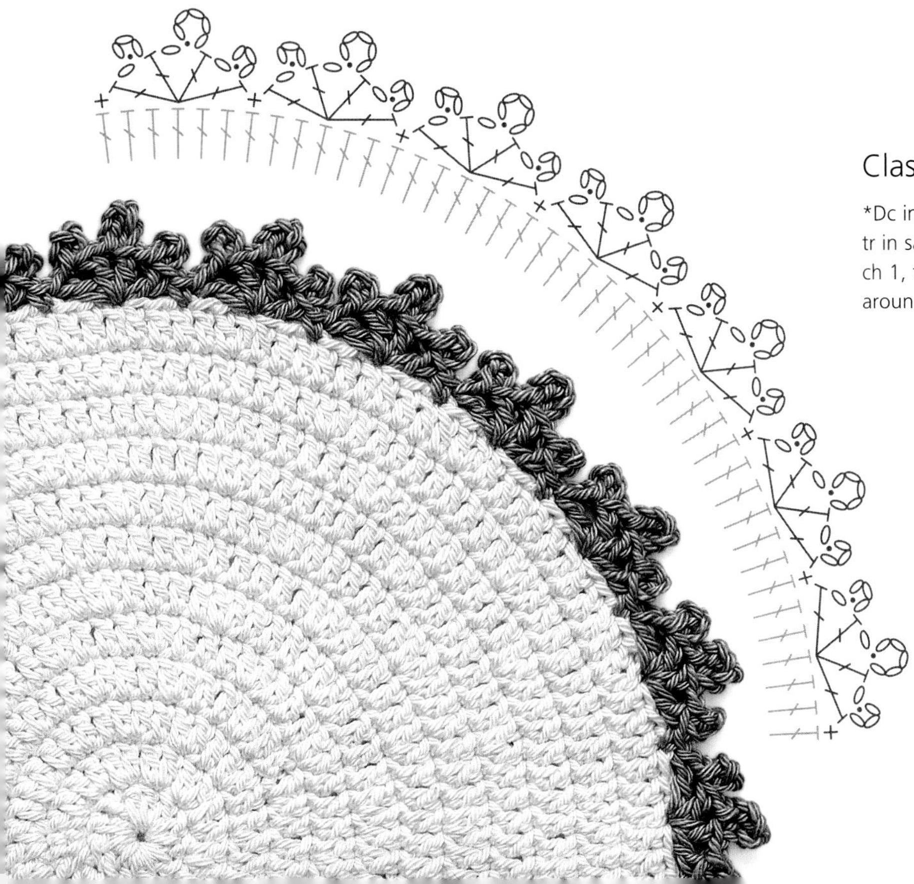

Classic Border

*Dc in st, skip next 2 sts, tr in next st, picot-3, ch 1, tr in same st, picot-5, ch 1, tr in same st, picot-3, ch 1, tr in same st, skip next 2 sts; rep from * all around. Join and weave in ends.

Chart Key   Special Stitches (see p.125)
+ dc   🖰 picot-3
Ŧ tr   🖰 picot-5
o ch

INSTRUCTIONS

Dandy Border

Round 1 (colour A): *Dc in st, picot-3, ch 1, skip next st; rep from * all around. Join.

Round 2 (colour B): This round is worked in last round of mandala, not in Round 1 of border. Work first st of this round over ch 1 of Round 1.

*Long dc in st of last round of mandala, ch 3 (behind picot-3 of Round 1); rep from * all around. Join and weave in ends.

You might have to pop the picots to the front of the work if they are caught behind Round 2.

Chart Key

+ dc
◯ ch

Special Stitch (see p.125)
🔟 picot-3

Coquette Border

Round 1 (colour A): *Dc in st, ch 3, skip next 2 sts; rep from * all around. Join.

Round 2: *Dc in dc, 5 tr in ch-3 sp; rep from * all around. Join.

Round 3 (colour B): *Long dc in dc of Round 1, dc in 5 tr; rep from * all around. Join and weave in ends.

Chart Key

+ dc
◯ ch
T tr

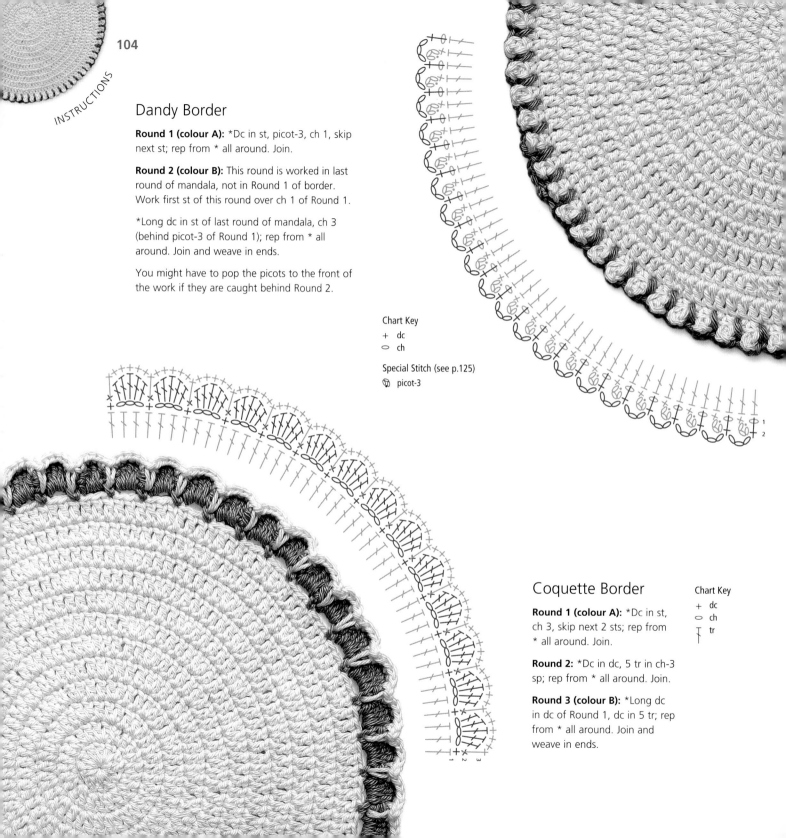

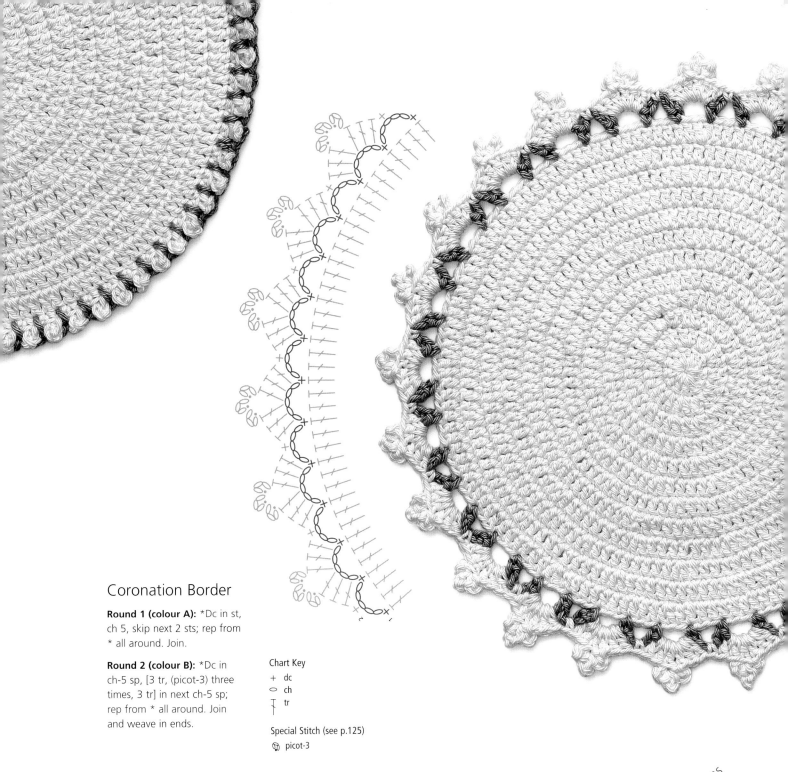

Coronation Border

Round 1 (colour A): *Dc in st, ch 5, skip next 2 sts; rep from * all around. Join.

Round 2 (colour B): *Dc in ch-5 sp, [3 tr, (picot-3) three times, 3 tr] in next ch-5 sp; rep from * all around. Join and weave in ends.

Chart Key

+ dc
○ ch
T tr

Special Stitch (see p.125)
🖏 picot-3

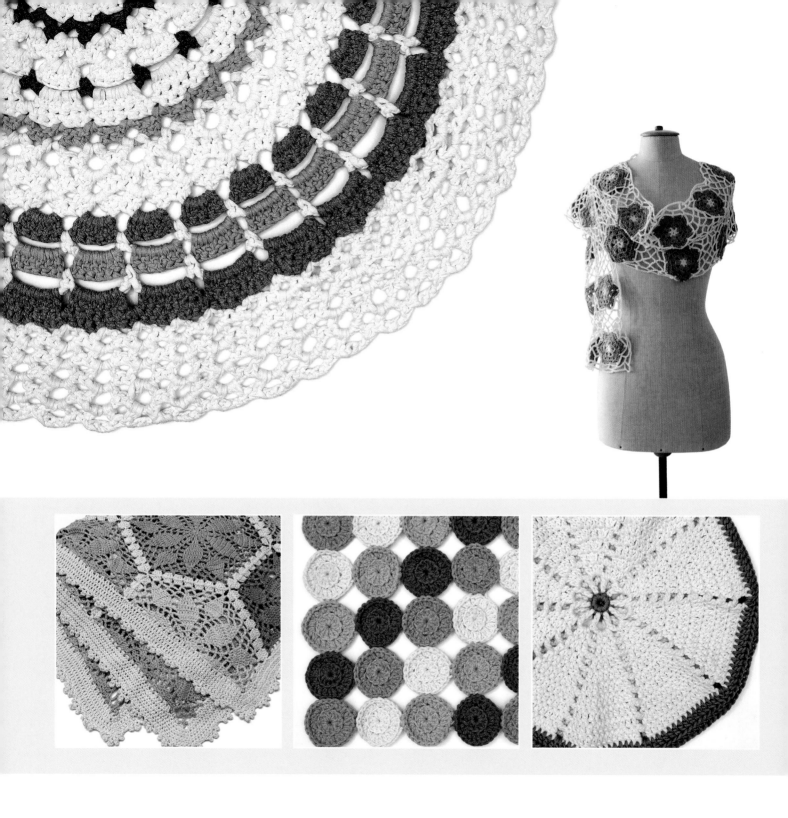

In this chapter we will take things a step further by turning some of the mandalas you mastered in the previous chapter into beautiful garments, accessories and homewares. Why not try substituting different mandala patterns for each project and experimenting with colour to create items that are truly unique?

PROJECTS

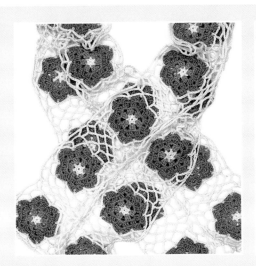

PROJECTS

BOHO BAG

This beautiful bohemian-style bag is made using the
'Pretty Pieces' mandala (see page 48).

6mm crochet hook

Chunky cotton yarn in
2 colours:
Colour A: 75m (82yd)
Colour B: 225m (246yd)

Yarn needle

Chart Key

- ◠ ch
- • sl st
- ⊤ tr
- ＋ dc
- Ⅴ tr2tog
- ◄ start of row

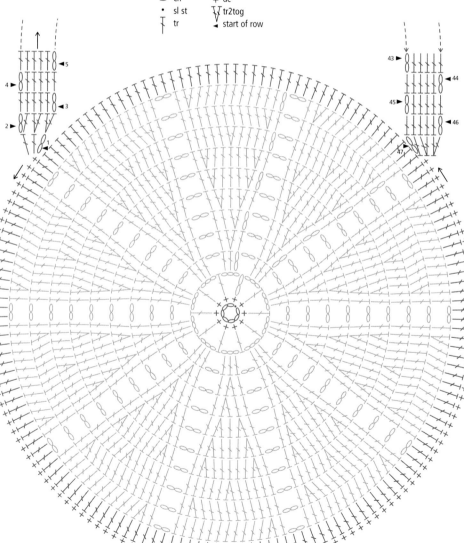

Front and Back

Make two 'Pretty Pieces' mandalas,
working Rounds 1–12 from the pattern
but omitting Round 13.

Joining front and back

Start this round in the first of 2 dc worked
in a ch-2 sp.

Hold front and back together, with right
sides facing. Work 1 dc through the inner
loops of both mandalas. Continue like this
around the mandalas until seven triangular
segments of the mandalas are joined. The
remaining three segments will form the
bag opening.

Shoulder Strap

Row 1: 3 tr in one corner of the bag
opening. Turn.

Row 2: 2 tr in each tr. You've now worked
6 tr in total; this will be the width of the
strap. Turn.

Row 3: Tr in each tr. Turn.

Rows 4–46: Repeat Row 3.

Row 47: Work these stitches in the other
corner of the bag opening, thus joining the
strap to that corner: [tr2tog] three times.

Fasten off.

Finishing touches

Turn the bag inside out and join the first
seven rows of the shoulder strap to the bag
on both sides by slip stitching or sewing.

HOTPAD

4.5mm crochet
hook

Aran-weight
non-mercerised
cotton yarn in
3 colours:
Colour A:
36.5m (40yd)
Colour B:
128m (140yd)
Colour C:
27.5m (30yd)

Yarn needle

Chart Key
⌐ ch
• sl st
† tr
◊ tr2tog
+ dc
◄ start of round

Special Stitch
(see p.125)
⌐ ttr = triple treble
crochet

This hotpad consists of two crocheted
mandalas pieced together in the final round
(Round 7). It is made with a medium-weight
yarn and 4.5mm crochet hook. A special
stitch used is the triple treble crochet.

Front

To start (colour A): Make a magic ring or ch 5 and
sl st in first ch to form a ring.

Round 1: 16 tr in ring. Join.

Round 2 (colour B): [Tr2tog in tr, ch 1] 16 times.
Join.

Round 3 (colour C): [3 tr in ch-1 sp] 16 times. Join.

Round 4 (colour A): *[Dc, ch 7, dc] between two
3-tr clusters, ch 4, dc in next sp between two 3-tr
clusters, ch 4; rep from * seven more times. Join.

Round 5: Start in any 2nd ch-4 sp. *Dc in ch-4 sp,
[6 tr, ch 2, 6 tr] in ch-7 sp, dc in ch-4 sp, ch 3;
rep from * seven more times. Join.

Round 6 (colour C): *Dc in ch-2 sp, ch 6, ttr in
ch-3 sp, ch 6; rep from * seven more times. Join.

Fasten off. Weave in ends.

Front

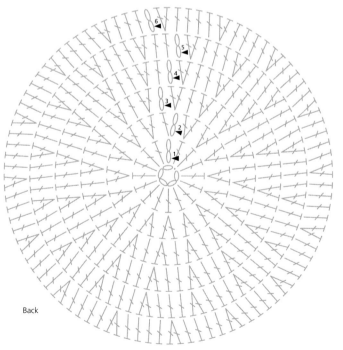

Back

Back

To start (colour B): Make a magic ring or ch 5 and sl st in first ch to form a ring.

Round 1: 16 tr in ring. Join.

Round 2: 2 tr in each st. Join.

Round 3: *Tr in st, 2 tr in next st; rep from * 16 times. Join.

Round 4: *Tr in 2 sts, 2 tr in next st; rep from * 16 times. Join.

Round 5: *Tr in 3 sts, 2 tr in next st; rep from * 16 times. Join.

Round 6: *Tr in 4 sts, 2 tr in next st; rep from * 16 times. Join.

Fasten off. Weave in ends.

Joining front and back
Place the two pieces together, the right side of the back facing the wrong side of the front. Work with the right side of the front facing you. Work every indicated stitch through the front and back mandalas.

Round 7: *Dc in ttr, 5 dc in ch-6 sp, dc in next dc, 5 dc in ch-6 sp; rep from * seven more times. Join. Fasten off. Weave in ends.

TIP Turn this hotpad into a potholder by crocheting a simple loop and securing it to your work with 1 dc.

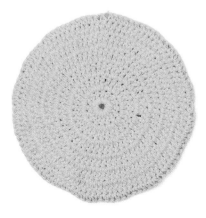

TABLEMAT

This tablemat is based on one of the classic mandalas: the 'Pebble in the Pond' mandala (see page 46). For this tablemat, I made 35 mini versions of the mandala in four colours. This tablemat is joined as you go, but, if you prefer, you can simply stitch them together at the end with a needle.

4.5mm crochet hook

Aran-weight non-mercerised cotton yarn in 4 colours: 45.75m (50yd) of each colour A–C and 41m (45yd) of colour D

Yarn needle (optional)

Make 35 mini 'Pebble in the Pond' mandalas in four colours as follows:

Colour A: 9 circles
Colour B: 9 circles
Colour C: 9 circles
Colour D: 8 circles

To start: Make a magic ring or ch 4 and sl st in first ch to form a ring.

Round 1: 12 tr in ring. Join.

Round 2: 2 BLtr in each st. Join.

Join as you go

Each mandala is joined to another with 2 tr. Join by working each connecting tr though both the circle you are making and through the back loop of the corresponding tr of the adjoining circle. Each circle is connected to a maximum of four other circles following this joining pattern:

4 regular tr, 2 joining tr, 4 regular tr, 2 joining tr, 4 regular tr, 2 joining tr, 4 regular tr, 2 joining tr.

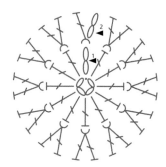

Chart Key
- ◯ ch
- • sl st
- ⊤ tr
- ⊤ BLtr
- ◀ start of round

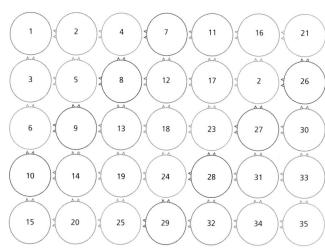

Placement of mandalas

SUMMER SCARF

The pattern for this light and sophisticated summer scarf is based on the first five rounds of the 'Rajasthan' mandala (see page 52).

4mm crochet hook

Fine-weight non-mercerised cotton yarn in 3 colours:
Colour A: 90m (98½yd)
Colour B: 1.8m (2yd)
Colour C: 7m (7½yd)
per motif

Yarn needle

To start (colour A): Make a magic ring or ch 4 and sl st in first ch to form a ring.

Round 1: 6 dc in ring. Join.

Round 2: [Sl st in st, ch 3] six times. Join.

Round 3 (colour B): [3 tr in ch-3 sp, ch 3] six times. Join.

Round 4 (colour C): *[3 tr, ch 2, 3 tr] in ch-3 sp; rep from * five more times. Join.

Round 5: *Dc in sp between clusters, [3 tr, ch 3, 3 tr] in ch-2 sp; rep from * five more times. Join.

Round 6 (colour A): *Dc in ch-3 sp, ch 5, skip 3 tr, dc in next dc, ch 5, skip 3 tr; rep from * five more times. Join.

Round 7: Ch 1, *dc in dc, ch 7, tr in next st, ch 7; rep from * four more times, dc in dc, ch 7, tr in next dc, ch 2, ttr in first dc of round. (This way you don't have to cut the yarn and will begin the next round exactly in the middle of a ch-7 sp as required.)

Round 8: Ch 1, *[dc, ch 7, dc] in ch-7 sp, ch 7, [ttr, ch 7, ttr] in next ch-7 sp (corner), ch 7; rep from * three more times. Join.

Fasten off. Weave in ends.

Make 24 motifs, or more if you'd like a longer or wider scarf.

Joining motifs

The motifs are joined as you work. Refer to the diagram for where the motifs are joined. They are joined with simple slip stitches. Be careful when joining that the motifs are arranged symmetrically.

Chart Key

◡ ch
• sl st
+ dc
⊤ tr
◄ start of round

Special Stitch (see p.125)

⊺ ttr = triple treble crochet

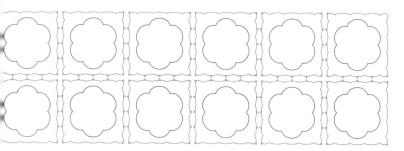

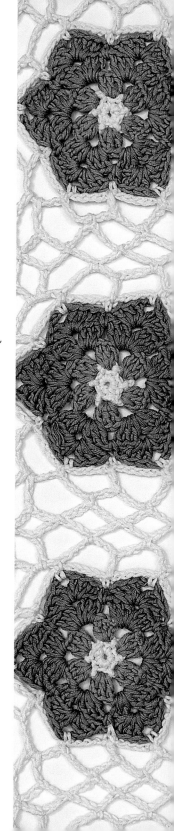

PROJECTS

LAP BLANKET

The basis for this blanket is formed by the first three rounds of the 'Make it Pop!' mandala (see page 68), with the third round slightly adapted. The example shown here consists of 94 motifs, but of course you can make it as big as you like. The motifs are joined as you go. I used all kinds of colours (except black) for this lap blanket, but only used pastels for every third round to ensure a harmonious result.

3mm crochet hook

Fine-weight mercerised cotton yarn in 3 colours:
Colour A: 1.25m (50in)
Colour B: 2m (80in)
Colour C: 6.4m (7yd)
per motif

Yarn needle

Chart Key
○ ch
• sl st
† tr
⟨⟩ tr2tog
◀ start of round

Special Stitches (see p.125)
pc = 5 tr popcorn

picot-5

To start (colour A): Make a magic ring or ch 5 and sl st in first ch to form a ring.

Round 1: [Tr in ring, ch 1] 12 times. Join.

Round 2 (colour B): [Tr2tog in ch-1 sp, ch 2] 12 times. Join.

Round 3 (colour C): *Pc in ch-2 sp, picot-5, ch 4; rep from * 11 more times. Join.

Joining motifs
Refer to the diagram and/or photo for where to join. The new motifs are joined in the third round when making the picot on top of the pc, as follows: ch 2, ch 1 in ch-5 sp of adjoining motif, ch 2, sl st in pc to close picot; continue pattern as usual and join as described where applicable.

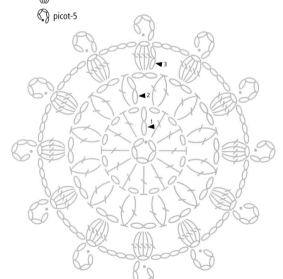

Placement of motifs

RUG

This rug is crocheted with a 10mm crochet hook using T-shirt yarn. The pattern is identical to that of the 'Marvellous Myriad' mandala (see page 60), but with a different colour plan.

10mm crochet hook

Super chunky T-shirt yarn in
4 colours:
Colour A: 480m (525yd)
Colour B: 20m (22yd)
Colour C: 70m (76½yd)
Colour D: 120m (131¼yd)

Large yarn needle

Colour A: White
Colour B: Charcoal grey
Colour C: Mint green
Colour D: Light grey

These are the colours used for the rug:

To start and Rounds 1–3: Colour A
Round 4: Colour B
Rounds 5–6: Colour A
Round 7: Colour B
Rounds 8–9: Colour A
Round 10: Colour C
Rounds 11–13: Colour A
Round 14: Colour D
Round 15: Colour A
Round 16: Colour C
Round 17: Colour A
Rounds 18–19: Colour D
Rounds 20–24: Colour A

LEAVES AND LACE BLANKET

For this blanket you need three motif patterns: the full motif (which is the 'Leaves and Lace' mandala from page 78, worked into a hexagon), plus two half-variants of this hexagon. We'll need these half-hexagons to fill in the sides of the blanket. Make all the required hexagons and half-hexagons first (Rounds 1–11), then (if you want to) block them. After that, you start adding Round 12, which is also the round where the motifs are joined. Use the diagram for the general layout for positioning of the motifs. The blanket is made out of 38 full motifs, 12 half-motifs A and 8 half-motifs B, plus a border. It's a big project but worth the effort!

4mm crochet hook

DK non-mercerised cotton yarn: 77.75m (85yd) coloured and 18.25m (20yd) white per motif

Yarn needle

Chart Key
⊖   ch
•   sl st
†   tr
⅄   tr2tog
⅄⅄   tr3tog
+   dc
◄   start of row

Special Stitches
(see p.125)
Ⓟ   picot-3
Ⓟ   picot-5

Leaves and Lace Hexagon
(full motif: make 38 in colours of your choice)

Rounds 1–11 (colour A): Work according to the 'Leaves and Lace' mandala on page 78.

Leaves and Lace Half-hexagon
(motif A: make 12)

To start (colour A): Make a magic ring or ch 4 and sl st in first ch to form a ring.

Row 1: Ch 3 (counts as tr, ch 1), [tr in ring, ch 1] five times, tr in ring. Turn.

Row 2: Ch 3 (counts as tr, ch 1), [2 tr in next tr, ch 1] six times, tr in next tr. Turn.

Row 3: Ch 2 (counts as tr), tr in same st, [ch 3, tr2tog, ch 3, tr in next tr, 2 tr in next tr] twice, ch 3, tr2tog, ch 3, 2 tr in next tr. Turn.

Row 4: Ch 2 (counts as tr), 2 tr in next tr, ch 3, [tr in next tr2tog, ch 3, 2 tr in next tr, tr in next tr, 2 tr in next tr, ch 3] twice, tr in next tr2tog, ch 3, 2 tr in next tr, tr in next tr. Turn.

Row 5: Ch 2 (counts as tr), tr in next tr, 2 tr in next tr, ch 3, tr in next tr, ch 3, [2 tr in next tr, tr in next tr, 2 tr in next tr, tr in next tr, 2 tr in next tr, ch 3, tr in next tr, ch 3] twice, 2 tr in next tr, tr in next 2 tr. Turn.

Row 6: Ch 2 (counts as tr), tr in next 3 tr, ch 3, *[tr, ch 3, tr] in next tr, ch 3, tr in next 8 tr, ch 3; rep from * once more, [tr, ch 3, tr] in next tr, ch 3, tr in next 4 tr. Turn.

Row 7: Ch 2 (counts as tr), tr in next tr, tr2tog, *ch 3, tr in next tr, 3 tr in ch-3 sp, tr in next tr, ch 3, tr2tog, tr in next 4 tr, tr2tog; rep from * once more, ch 3, tr in next tr, 3 tr in ch-3 sp, tr in next tr, ch 3, tr2tog, tr in next 2 sts. Turn.

Row 8: Ch 2 (counts as tr), tr2tog, ch 5, *[2 tr in next tr, tr in next tr] twice, 2 tr in next tr, ch 5, tr2tog**, tr in next 2 tr, tr2tog, ch 5; rep from * once more, then rep from * to ** once, tr in last st. Turn.

Row 9: Standing tr2tog, ch 5, dc in ch-5 sp, *ch 5, [tr2tog, tr in next tr] twice, tr2tog, ch 5, dc in ch-5 sp, ch 5**, [tr2tog] twice, ch 5, dc in ch-5 sp; rep from * once more, then rep from * to ** once, tr2tog. Turn.

Row 10: Ch 7 (counts as tr, ch 5), dc in ch-5 sp, ch 5, dc in ch-5 sp, *ch 5, tr2tog, tr in next tr, tr2tog, [ch 5, dc in ch-5 sp] twice, ch 5, tr2tog, [ch 5, dc in ch-5 sp] twice**; rep from * once more, then rep from * to ** once, ch 5, tr in last st. Turn.

Row 11: [Ch 5, dc in ch-5 sp] three times, ch 5, tr3tog, [ch 5, dc in ch-5 sp] six times, ch 5, tr3tog, [ch 5, dc in ch-5 sp] six times, ch 5, tr3tog, [ch 5, dc in ch-5 sp] three times, ch 3, tr in last st.

Fasten off. Weave in ends.

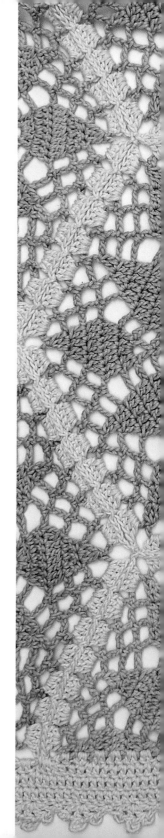

Leaves and Lace Half-hexagon (motif B: make 8)

To start: Make a magic ring or ch 4 and sl st in first ch to form a ring.

Row 1: Ch 3 (counts as tr, ch 1), [tr in ring, ch 1] six times, tr in ring. Turn.

Row 2: Ch 3 (counts as tr, ch 1), [2 tr in next tr, ch 1] five times, tr in next tr. Turn.

Row 3: Ch 5 (counts as tr, ch 3), [tr in next tr, 2 tr in next tr, ch 3, tr2tog, ch 3] twice, tr in next tr, 2 tr, ch 3, tr in last tr. Turn.

Row 4: Ch 5 (counts as tr, ch 3), *2 tr in next tr, tr in next tr, 2 tr in next tr, ch 3, tr in next tr**, ch 3; rep from * once more, then rep from * to ** once. Turn.

Row 5: Ch 5 (counts as tr, ch 3), [(2 tr in next tr, tr in next tr) twice, 2 tr in next tr, ch 3, tr in next tr, ch 3] twice, [2 tr in next tr, tr in next tr] twice, 2 tr in next tr, ch 3, tr in next tr. Turn.

Row 6: Ch 3 (counts as tr, ch 1), tr in same st, *ch 3, tr in next 8 sts, ch 3**, [tr, ch 3, tr] in next st; rep from * once more, then rep from * to ** once, [tr, ch 1, tr] in last st. Turn.

Row 7: Ch 2 (counts as tr), tr in ch-1 sp, tr in next tr, *ch 3, tr2tog, tr in next 4 tr, tr2tog, ch 3, tr in next tr**, 3 tr in ch-3 sp, tr in next tr; rep from * once more, then from * to ** once, tr in ch-1 sp, tr in last st. Turn.

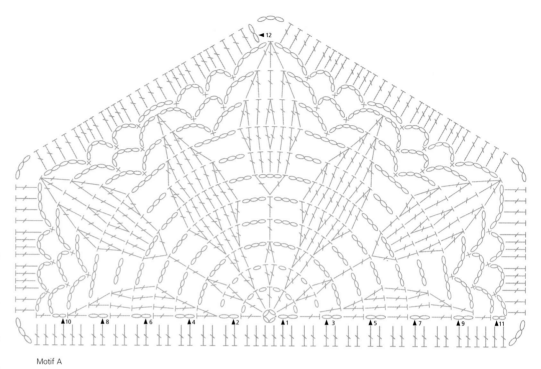

Motif A

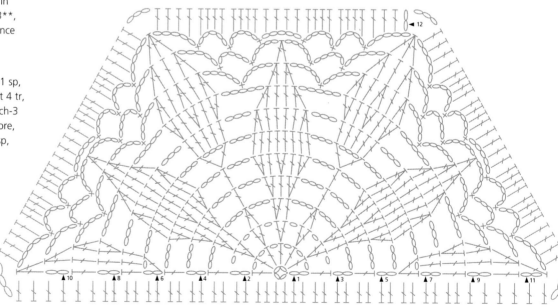

Motif B

Row 8: Ch 2 (counts as tr), tr in next tr, 2 tr in next tr, *ch 5, tr2tog, tr in next 2 tr, tr2tog, ch 5**, [2 tr in next tr, tr in next tr] twice, 2 tr in next tr; rep from * once more, then rep from * to ** once, 2 tr in next tr, tr in next 2 sts. Turn.

Row 9: Ch 2 (counts as tr), tr in next tr, tr2tog, ch 5, dc in ch-5 sp, *ch 5, [tr2tog] twice, ch 5, dc in ch-5 sp, ch 5**, [tr2tog, tr in next tr] twice, tr2tog, ch 5, dc in ch-5 sp; rep from * once more, then rep from * to ** once, tr2tog, tr in next 2 sts. Turn.

Row 10: Ch 2 (counts as tr), tr2tog, [ch 5, dc in ch-5 sp] twice, *ch 5, tr2tog, [ch 5, dc in ch-5 sp] twice, ch 5**, tr2tog, tr in next tr, tr2tog, [ch 5, dc in ch-5 sp] twice; rep from * once more, then rep from * to ** once, tr2tog, tr in final st. Turn.

Row 11: Standing tr2tog, [ch 5, dc in ch-5 sp] six times, ch 5, tr3tog, [ch 5, dc in ch-5 sp] six times, ch 5, tr3tog, [ch 5, dc in ch-5 sp] six times, ch 5, tr2tog.

Fasten off. Weave in ends.

Joining motifs
The motifs are joined while working Round 12.

Full motif
Start round in the first ch-5 sp after the tr3tog of Round 11 and work as follows: [4 tr in each of next 7 ch-5 sps, ch 3] six times. Join.

Half-hexagons
For the sides, follow the pattern as described above for the full motif. For the long underside: work 2 tr in each tr, plus 2 tr in the centre (the magic ring or ch 4 that is at the centre of the half-hexagons) – a total of 46 tr.

Where the motifs are joined, sl st between each pair of corresponding 4-tr clusters along the side of the adjoining motif. In the ch-3 corners,

three motifs will be joined together by replacing 2 ch of the ch-3 corner with a sl st in each of the two adjoining motifs. Where only two motifs join at a ch-3 corner, replace 1 ch with a sl st in the adjoining motif.

Border

The border is based on the Classic Border as described on page 103, but for this blanket I made it wider and adapted it by adding corners.

Round 1: This round straightens the sides of the blanket. Depending on the yarn you've used and your style of crocheting, you might have to switch to a slightly smaller or bigger hook to prevent your blanket from either ruffling or becoming too tight.

Work the round as follows: tr in each tr along sides, 2 tr in each of the two ch sps where motifs join along sides, 3 tr in each of the four ch-3 corners.

Round 2: Tr in each tr, except in the corners where you work 3 tr in the middle st of the 3-tr corner of previous round.

Round 3: Repeat Round 2.

If you'd like a wider border, repeat this round as many times as desired.

Round 4: *Dc, skip next 2 sts, [tr, picot-3, ch 1, picot-5, ch 1, tr, picot-3, ch 1, tr] in same st, skip next 2 sts**; rep from * to corner. Join.

In each corner adapt the pattern as follows: [(tr, picot-3, ch 1) twice, tr, picot-5, ch 1, (tr, picot-3, ch 1) twice, tr] all in same st, skip next 2 sts; continue the pattern as described between * and ** to next corner. Join.

Fasten off. Weave in ends.

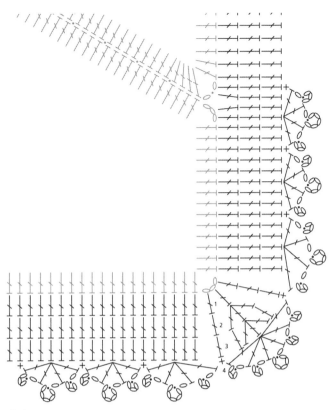

Border

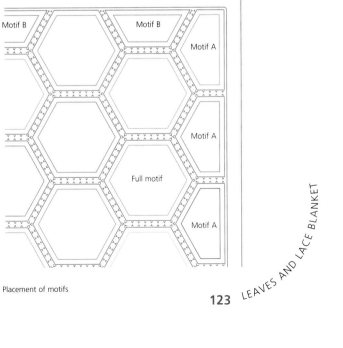

Placement of motifs

SYMBOLS AND ABBREVIATIONS

These are the abbreviations and symbols that are used in this book. There is no worldwide standard, so in other publications you may find different abbreviations and symbols. Throughout this book, English crochet terms are used. Always remember that a chart represents how a stitch pattern is constructed and may not always bear much resemblance to the appearance of the finished piece. Always read the written instructions together with the chart.

English/American equivalent terms

Some American terms differ from the English system, as shown below. Patterns you may encounter that are published using American terminology can be very confusing unless you understand the difference.

Symbol	English	American	American abbreviation
+	double crochet	single crochet	sc
 T	half treble	half double	hdc
 †	treble	double	dc
 ‡	double treble	treble	tr
 ‡	triple treble	double treble	dtr
 ‡	sextuple treble	quintuple treble	quintr

Common Stitches, Symbols and Abbreviations

These are the basic crochet stitches that appear in most of the mandalas in this book. For step-by-step instructions for working all of these stitches and techniques, see pages 20–24.

Ch Chain stitch

Sl st Slip stitch

Dc Double crochet

Htr Half treble crochet

Tr Treble crochet

Dtr Double treble crochet

BL Work stitch through the back loop only

FL Work stitch through the front loop only

Tr2tog Treble crochet two together

Tr3tog Treble crochet three together

Tr4tog Treble crochet four together

Dtr3tog Double treble crochet three together

Special Stitches

In addition to the basic stitches, some of the mandalas use special stitches that might be a bit more complex or that you may not have come across before. Where these occur in the book, the abbreviation is indicated in the special stitch listing, near to the chart key.

 Ttr (triple treble crochet): [Yo] three times, insert hook in indicated st, yo and pull up a loop, [yo, pull through two loops on hook] four times.

 Crab stitch: Also known as reverse double crochet. Working from left to right, insert hook in next st to right, yo, pull loop through, yo, pull through both loops on hook.

 Pc (5-tr popcorn): Use whichever method you prefer:

METHOD A: 5 tr in indicated st or space, remove hook from loop and reinsert (from front to back) in top of first of the 5 tr, pick up live loop and draw through first tr, ch 1 to secure popcorn.

METHOD B: 5 tr in indicated st or space, turn work (leaving loop on hook) and insert hook in first tr, yo, pull through the first tr and through the loop on hook, turn work so that front is facing you again and continue.

 Picot-3: Ch 3, sl st in first ch.

 Picot-4: Ch 4, sl st in first ch.

 Picot-5: Ch 5, sl st in first ch.

 Puff stitch: [Yo, insert hook where required and draw through a loop] three times in the same place. You now have seven loops on the hook. Yo and pull through all loops.

FPhtr (front post half treble crochet): Yo and insert hook from front to back, around post of st in row below from right to left, and back to front of work. Yo and pull up loop. Yo and pull through all loops on hook.

 FPtr (front post treble crochet) (see also page 22): Yo and insert hook from front to back of work, around post of st in row below from right to left, and through to front again. Yo and pull up loop. [Yo and pull through two loops on hook] twice.

 FPdtr (front post double treble crochet): [Yo] twice, insert hook from front to back of work, around post of st in row below from right to left, and through to front again. Yo and pull up loop. [Yo and pull through two loops on hook] three times.

 FPquadtr (front post quadruple treble crochet): [Yo] four times, insert hook from front to back of work, around post of st in row below from right to left, and through to front again. Yo and pull up loop. [Yo and pull through two loops on hook] five times.

FPsextr (front post sextuple treble crochet): [Yo] six times, insert hook from front to back of work, around post of st in row below from right to left, and through to front again. Yo and pull up loop. [Yo and pull through two loops on hook] seven times.

BPhtr (back post half treble crochet): Yo and insert hook from back to front of work, around post of st in row below from right to left, and through to back again. Yo and pull up loop. Yo and pull through all loops on hook.

BPtr (back post treble crochet) (see also page 22): Yo and insert hook from back to front of work, around post of st in row below from right to left, and through to back again. Yo and pull up loop. [Yo and pull through two loops on hook] twice.

Db lp (double loop stitch): The basis of the double loop st is a dc but with little tweaks to make the loops. Wrap yarn over index finger of your left hand (if you are right-handed) twice. Insert hook in next st, wrap hook around working yarn in opposite direction to normal (anticlockwise) and insert hook behind two strands of yarn on your finger, and pull them from behind your index finger, then draw them and the working yarn (three loops in total) through the stitch. You now have four loops on the hook. Continue as a regular dc: yo and draw yarn through all loops on hook. Let two loops slide off index finger. When two double loop stitches are required, the symbol is shown in a 'V'.

INDEX

CREDITS

All step-by-step and other images are the copyright of Quarto Publishing plc. While every effort has been made to credit contributors, Quarto would like to apologise should there have been any omissions or errors – and would be pleased to make the appropriate correction for future editions of the book.

Author Acknowledgements

My sincere thanks to the lovely people at Quarto for a wonderful co-operation: Lily de Gatacre, Kate Kirby, Jackie Palmer, Victoria Lyle, Julia Shone and Georgia Cherry – and, of course, the rest of this splendid team. Their eye for even the smallest details made it a joy to make this book. Also, I'd like to thank my Instagram friends @elisabethandree and @marretjeroos for their valued input.

Many thanks to DMC Creative who generously supplied yarn for many of the mandalas in this book and the Summer Scarf project on pages 114–115.

For DMC crochet threads (Natura), patterns etc.

DMC Creative World Ltd
Unit 21 Warren Park Way
Warrens Park, Enderby
Leicester LE19 4SA
UNITED KINGDOM
+44 116 275 4000

www.dmccreative.co.uk

We would also like to thank Scaapi who generously supplied the hand-dyed Vinnis Nikkim yarn for the Leaves and Lace Blanket on pages 120–123.

Scaapi
Oranjelaan 33
3971 HD
Driebergen
NETHERLANDS
+31 6-10218073

www.scaapi.nl
info@scaapi.nl

The following colours of yarn have been used in this book:

DMC Natura Just Cotton
N02 Ivory, N03 Sable, N04 Ambar, N05 Bleu Layette, N06 Rose Layette, N07 Spring Rose, N09 Gris Argent, N10 Aswan, N12 Light Green, N18 Coral, N19 Topaze, N29 Lazuite, N35 Nacar, N44 Agatha, N47 Safran, N48 Chartreuse, N49 Turquoise, N50 Parme, N51 Erica, N52 Geranium, N56 Azur, N64 Prussian, N79 Tilleul, N78 Lin, N82 Lobelia, N85 Giroflée, N87 Glacier.

Vinnis Nikkim Hand-dyed 100% Cotton
Natural-500, Camel-504, Pale Blue-Green-518, Pale Sage-519, Pink-521, Ballet Pink-522, Purple Pink-525, Avocado-530, Baby Blue-534, Sunshine-535, Baby Yellow-536, Stone-541, Dunes-545, Mint-554, Peach-558, Turquoise-564, Pale Khaki-570, Tomato-575, Blue-Grey-577, Sand-578, Burnt-Orange-581, Pale Lilac-587, Kingfisher-591.

Please use the above list as a guide only and be sure to check exact colours with your yarn supplier before purchasing.